Pick Up the Phone

Creating a Culture that Establishes Meaningful Relationships with Students

Andrew J. Mills

Pick Up the Phone:
Creating a Culture that Establishes
Meaningful Relationships with Students

Contact: andrew@millsmentality.com

Table of Contents

Introduction: Who's On the Other End?............................i

1 Finding Your Source 1

2 When People, Processes, and
   Procedures Get in the Way 19

3 Will Power: Why Not You?....................................... 33

4 Becoming a Student Again...................................... 43

5 Pouring from an Empty Cup 53

6 Teaching vs. Learning.. 65

7 Shorts in the Circuit to Success............................. 75

8 Remembering the Past: Learning the Hard Way 87

9 The Dash Effect... 97

10 It's Not What We Say, It's What We Do..................... 109

11 You Don't Have to Be Seen to Be Heard 121

12 Creatures of Habit: Caring More
   About the Future 131

13 Simple Math: You + Them
   & Conversation > Consequence............................ 145

14 Parents, Educators, Students:
   Moving in the Same Direction 163

15 Calculated Communication:
   Creating a Healthy Dialogue 177

16 Building a Culture of Care 189

17 Right Voices, Right Choices:
   Letting Students Speak 199

18 Everybody Wins, but
   Everybody Doesn't Get a Trophy 209

Conclusion: Pick Up the Phone!............................... 217

DEDICATION

This book is dedicated to all those who have embraced one of the noblest professions our country has to offer—that of the educator.

By answering the call to serve in education, you have been given the opportunity to make a positive impact on the lives of your students. You have the power to make a difference.

It all begins when you simply *Pick Up the Phone*.

ACKNOWLEDGEMENTS

Thank you to my mother, Jennifer Sullivan. You always have been, and continue to be, my #1 fan! It is because of your support and encouragement that I am living my dream.

Thank you to Dr. Rod and Joni Parsley for providing the opportunity for me to fulfill my life's purpose on earth. Your commitment to education has changed the lives of so many students.

Thank you to Mr. Trocchia for epitomizing what it means to be an educator. You challenged me to exceed the standard. Your commitment to excellence in education is what I strive to emulate today.

Thank you to Shannon Lee for inspiring me to become a better servant leader. Thank you for your mentorship and for challenging me to defy the norm.

Thank you to my colleagues for putting up with my out-of-the-box methods. Your support in our quest to create the best school in the world is truly encouraging. We have embarked on a journey that will not only impact our students, but will change our lives forever!

Last, but not least, thank you to the hundreds and hundreds of students I have encountered in my 14 years in education. To students like Gideon, Sean, and Judah who showed me it was okay to just be me in the classroom: you made teaching worth it! To students like Daniel, Elijah, and Jesse who challenged me to think beyond the status quo to create innovative experiences for so many students: you made being a principal worth it!

INTRODUCTION

Who's On the Other End?

As educators, we are often encouraged—and even expected—to build relationships with our students. In many cases, there is no clear guidance on how to make this happen.

We have already learned that much of what we encounter during the school day was never taught in college, so how can we possibly learn the fundamentals of building relationships with all the different types of learners and personalities that we encounter in our classrooms? Truth be told, most of us are still trying to figure out how to actually differentiate our instruction!

It's hard enough to juggle the various responsibilities that come with teaching. Most tasks that we have to complete usually come with some level of stress and what seems like an unreasonable deadline. Despite the challenges and arbitrary expectations placed on us, I firmly believe that when we fully and wholly understand what it takes to truly educate a student, we can then achieve a level of liberating freedom for ourselves, while also meeting the needs of the student.

When we want to communicate exciting or important news to someone, the first thing we typically do is pick up our phones and make a call. Our purpose is to effectively communicate our message to the person on the other end. No matter what news is being communicated, our goal is to get that news into the ears of the other person, and get their reaction to it.

Think about who is on the other end of what we do as educators: our students! Our students are the recipients of not only our instruction, but our attitudes, aptitudes, and our many moods. For the overwhelming majority of us, students were the main reason we chose this career path.

The satisfaction we receive when a student achieves a proverbial "Aha!" moment cannot be matched, especially when we have worked long and hard on lesson-planning. When our students score well on the unit test for a topic we felt was challenging to teach, it makes our efforts all worthwhile.

Every student is different; every teacher is different. Every student needs to be treated individually; every teacher needs that as well. The day of the "one-size-fits-all" lesson plan is long gone—for both teacher and student. It is our assignment now to take the time necessary to learn about each of our students, and to create plans to meet their needs.

Too often, we stress ourselves out when students don't respond to a lesson in the way we envisioned they would. Often, it's because we design lessons with *us* in mind, not *them*. Just because something seems fun, or because it worked for another teacher, doesn't mean that it's what is best for our students. If we began to truly dissect what it is our students needed and then integrated that into our content standards, we would be better able to achieve authentic success. We would learn to shift the focus to *who* is on the other end of our instruction.

As you read this book—a manifesto of sorts with tips and ideas for building relationships with students—I hope you will become inspired. I hope this book will not only challenge you, but that it will give you the courage to try something new. No matter how small or trivial something might sound, when you shift your mindset and put forth the effort all in the name of student success, you will have the opportunity to reach a level of satisfaction that will motivate you for years to come.

Andrew J. Mills
Middle/High School Principal
Harvest Preparatory School
Canal Winchester, Ohio

Chapter One

Finding Your Source

"**M**r. Mills, I can't believe I got an A on this test! It must've been easier than your other tests!"

One of the students in the freshman world history class I taught several years ago was excited about his score on the unit test I was passing back. Knowing the format was exactly the same as the last test—multiple choice, true and false, and short answer questions—I asked Alex why he thought the test was easier.

"I'm not really sure, but I actually studied this time."

While I was thrilled that he took my test seriously for once, what he said next made me chuckle, because he was being more profound than he realized.

"Just imagine what my grade would look like if I studied for every test!"

FUNCTIONING AT FULL POTENTIAL

The conclusion that Alex came to after seeing his test result was significant, and much more complex than he realized.

Imagine, for a moment, if every time we picked up our cell phones, they only operated at 50% functionality—regardless of the time of day or the urgency with which we needed to search for something on the Internet. What if, when we needed to make a post on social media, we discovered that the app only worked 50% of the time?

What would happen if our refrigerators only kept our food cold 50% of the time? How would we function today if the electricity in our homes only worked 50% of the time? Without the power and appropriate mechanisms for these items to function at their full capacities, the landscape of our lives would be drastically changed.

For a student, a score of 50% is considered failing. If a student only earns half of the possible points on an assignment or assessment, it suggests that only half of the information taught has been assimilated.

There are always reasons a student earns a low score. The student may have been unprepared for the test because they didn't study in an effective manner—or even study at all.

The student may have fallen short due to our method of instruction. Every student learns in a different way. We are responsible for developing a plan for each student so that they all end up at the same location and with the same result, keeping in mind that the time and manner in which each student achieves mastery of our content can and will vary.

There are also other underlying physiological and emotional needs which, if not understood or met, might create a culture that prevents the student from finding success in the classroom. They are falling short of the opportunity for maximum growth in their educational experience.

Whatever the cause, the student was not functioning at their full potential.

For an educator, not giving 100% effort in the classroom means we aren't functioning at our full capacity. Our interactions with our students and peers will be impacted.

Sometimes, like Alex, we have to make adjustments when we realize we're not functioning at our full potential. It's important to adapt and overcome. What that might look like for each person is different. For Alex, it meant studying for a test. For us, it might be an increased awareness of what we could accomplish and how we could motivate our students when we ourselves are striving for a high level of output.

We've all seen those memes or images of a person tunneling their way through a mountain, hitting the point of exhaustion and giving up, only to discover that they were right at the point of breaking through to the other side.

Once we set out on a journey, every step we take is one step farther away from the starting line and one step closer to the finish line. In order to win a race, we can't go backwards to the starting line; we must move forward to the finish line. Even when obstacles get in our way, we must keep our eyes on the prize and keep pushing forward. We can all attest that there is no greater feeling than setting a goal and achieving it, especially when we have navigated successfully through adversity. When we encounter challenging times or situations, we must keep our end goal in mind.

Think of a traffic detour. We dread those orange cones and barrels, but if we put our faith in the process and follow the signs, we will eventually reach our intended location. And through that process, we are opened to new experiences that wouldn't have been available along our normal route.

Have you ever noticed during an awards show that those who win always thank those who helped them along the way? Although these people might be a diverse group of friends, family, producers, co-stars, writers, or various others, they are those who were a source of motivation and strength which allowed the winners to achieve greatness.

We have all known people who motivated us and challenged us to achieve more than we ever thought possible. Who are those people for you? Can you identify those who have helped you find your way through life?

We will all go through experiences that exhaust us or lead to burnout during the school year. These instances may be issues with students, uncooperative parents, or even school administrators who don't support our initiatives in the classroom.

When we sense ourselves reaching the point of burnout, we are at risk of becoming complacent in our instruction and even in our relationships with colleagues and students. Complacency can become addictive. It's easy to sit by and allow cynicism and negativity to set in, which doesn't bode well for the classroom environment. We must find a source that keeps us moving forward and that keeps our zeal alive so we can continue to be productive and execute with passion in the classroom.

Much like an electronic device that requires power to operate, we, too, must be connected to a source that provides the needed energy for us to effectively motivate and inspire our students. Based on our personal and professional experiences and goals, that source will look different for each of us. Think of your source as the energy that keeps you going. Think of it as the electricity that keeps your light burning. Think of it as the reason you chose to become an educator in the first place.

HOW ARE YOU WIRED?

When it comes to finding our source of motivation, it's imperative that we take a look at both intrinsic and extrinsic factors. While we typically are wired with a dominant motivation, we can possess traits of both.

I liken being wired intrinsically to being wired with the qualitative value in mind and being wired extrinsically with the quantitative value in mind.

Intrinsic wiring focuses on the internal satisfaction and fulfillment that is attained at the completion of an activity. We engage in the activity because we enjoy doing it.

Examples of intrinsic wiring could include finding the learning experience in every opportunity, or the feeling we get when a student finally achieves their "Aha!" moment in class.

Extrinsic wiring focuses on the external rewards or recognition received as a result of completing a task. We are motivated by the end result or the prize earned.

Examples of extrinsic wiring might include keeping score and working toward an "Employee of the Quarter" recognition or highlighting the fact that 100% of our students earned a proficient score on their math speed drills.

As a school principal, I have experienced elements of being both intrinsically and extrinsically wired. Personally, I can find my energy in talking with or counseling a student through a challenging situation. But professionally, I can also find motivation by focusing on statistics—seeing how our school is rated and ranked in comparison to other comparable schools. Knowing how I am wired helps me to be as close to 100% as possible for my students.

Understanding how we are wired personally will help us understand what behaviors trigger certain responses in our professional life. It is important to understand the difference between intrinsic and extrinsic wiring because we will face a classroom full of students with many differing personalities, traits, and motivations. Once we know how we are wired personally, we then have to translate that into our profession as an educator, keeping in mind all the factors we will encounter at school.

Your students probably don't fully understand how they're wired yet, so we must be cognizant of the fact that *we* might be their source of motivation. In some cases, we might be their *only* source of motivation. The atmosphere we create in our classrooms might be the determining factor in whether or not a student completes their homework or even comes to school.

If our students feel they are being treated fairly, that might be the needed encouragement for them to make it through the school day. We might be the laugh or the fist bump that gives a student the hope they need to face their living situation when they get off the bus later that afternoon. The trust we establish might even be the source of inspiration that helps a student change their perspective on building relationships both with their peers and with the adults in their lives.

The realization that we can become a source for our students becomes the bridge or the catalyst for creating a relationship. Some standard buzzwords and phrases that are common and often over-used for educators regarding instructional practices include *differentiation, flipped classroom model,* and *blended learning.* While instructional practices and models are essential for student growth, we must not move too quickly and forget that there are underlying concepts which are necessary to make these educational practices work.

These concepts include *holistic education, relationships,* and even simple precepts that make a big difference, such as *caring* and *empathy.* We frequently hear about how important it is to build relationships, but admittedly, we don't know best practices for doing so. Often, we don't even know how to begin that process.

In the beginning stages of building relationships, there are always dynamics that have to be considered. Students often crave the affection and attention of their teachers. We must work to give them the attention they need in a professional way, because our goal for them should be their success.

The kind of attention we give them will vary, based on what it is they need in order to achieve success. Every student is going to ask for attention in a different way. And often, they won't even use words.

When we look at a beautiful tapestry hanging on a wall, we are usually impressed by the view of the front side. What we often overlook is the back side, which might be crisscrossed with what looks like a disarray of various colored threads and knots. But each thread serves a specific purpose and is a necessary part of the overall design.

In order for our students to parallel the completed image on the front, we have to work every single day to fully understand the behaviors and life experiences of our students. Our student's lives are like the back side of the tapestry—an intricate collection of experiences and influences that make up who they are. When we seek to understand and meet our students at their level, we can provide the guidance and leadership in order to begin to meet their academic needs.

Students will spend an average of 6 hours of their day in our classrooms, which means there are 18 hours of time in which they are in a completely different environment. No matter how hard we work to create positive learning outcomes for our students, the opportunity for them to be influenced by other people—whether in a good or a bad way—might trump our efforts. This does not mean that we should stop creating memories or learning experiences that provoke our students to achieve more and to think critically for themselves, but it does mean that we should be aware of the other influences in their lives.

We would be naïve to assume that our students come to us each day ready to learn. As adults, there are still times when we simply can't function on the job and need to use personal time to get our affairs in order. It is the same for our students: no matter their age, they come to us with their own sets of issues.

THE TWO DIFFERENT TYPES OF STUDENTS

Let's look at Sarah and Michelle, two hypothetical students, to get a better understanding of why students in our classrooms might act the way they do. Understanding what motivates us will help us understand what motivates them. The more we understand about why students behave as they do, the better able we will be to assess and meet their educational needs.

Sarah

Sarah lives with her mother and father, both of whom are college graduates and work in leadership roles within their career fields. Sarah's mother always ensures that dinner is made as soon as she gets home from work. Sarah's father always helps her with her homework and makes sure she reads for 30 minutes each night.

Before bed, Sarah lays her clothes out for the next day, and places them next to her book bag that holds her finished homework. At bedtime, her mother lies in bed next to her and runs through Sarah's list of spelling words before kissing her goodnight and turning out the light. Sarah gets a full eight hours of sleep each night, wakes up to a bowl of cereal, grabs her packed lunch and book bag, and hops into her father's SUV to be driven to school.

Michelle

Michelle lives with her mother and three younger siblings. Her mother works as a receptionist during the day. She also works as a waitress three evenings each week. Michelle's father is absent from her life apart from his custody responsibilities on major holidays. He lives in a different state.

Because her mother's second job is a part-time evening shift, Michelle is left to tend to the needs of her younger siblings on those days. When she gets off the bus in the afternoon, she warms up the dinner that her mother left in the refrigerator before she went to her first job early that morning. Then, she helps her siblings with their homework, makes sure they take their baths, and tucks them into bed. If she has the energy, she will work on some of her own homework.

In the morning, Michelle's mother wakes them all up, and prepares herself for work while Michelle deals with the usual mayhem of getting everyone dressed and out the door to the bus stop. Some days they will have time to eat breakfast, other days they won't. Thankfully, the family qualifies for the free or reduced meal program, so

Michelle's mother knows they will at least receive a breakfast and a hot lunch every day at school.

If a student like Sarah comes to school prepared and ready to engage in the learning process—with their physiological needs met—chances are she will perform better academically and behave in accordance with classroom expectations.

When a student like Michelle comes into the classroom, she is strongly focused on her own survival. Michelle should be free to concentrate on academic success, but instead, she is burdened with handling a weight of responsibility that is beyond the maturity of her years.

Such a burden would cause any child to seek attention from her teachers. But, as is often the case, the attention-seeking behavior we see from this type of student is negative rather than positive. How can we expect a student living under such circumstances to come to school prepared and ready to engage in the learning process?

What happens when a student fails to receive any positive affirmations from any adults during their day? Let's say Michelle's mother is frustrated with her and the other children in the morning because they didn't have their clothes ready, so she expresses her irritation as they walk out the door and head to the bus stop. As Michelle gets on the bus, the driver just stares at her and doesn't greet her as she makes her way to her seat. Once she arrives at school, her teacher starts fussing at her because she didn't move her marker to the appropriate color to show she was present for the day. When she gets to the cafeteria for lunch, she discovers she is ten cents short, and the cashier tells her this is the last time she can charge, and the next infraction means she won't be able to eat.

This scenario paints a picture of a student who is working against a deficit of positive interaction. Because we might be the only source of encouragement our students will encounter during the day, we must become more intentional about our communication and our interactions with them.

We should strive to come to work at 100%. While that might not be realistically possible, we should certainly strive to be at our very best. If we only function at 50% all the time, there is no way our students will be able to achieve their best academically.

Students sense our level of excitement and passion. If they see that we're frustrated, then they are going to be nervous about making us even more frustrated. That does not create a healthy environment for them to learn, and their ability to function at 100% effort becomes greatly diminished.

I think we can agree that it's not humanly possible for a teacher to show up at school and teach every lesson flawlessly. But when we understand our internal wiring, it helps us possess the intrinsic or extrinsic fuel we need to keep pushing and striving for excellence even when we miss the mark. Perfection isn't possible, but when we are operating and functioning at our very best and using maximum effort, we become infused with the power necessary to create change in the lives of our students.

Every single interaction, no matter how small or trivial, plays a significant role and can become more meaningful to our students than we realize, especially when it comes to how we use our words. We may not remember the exact words people use in their interactions with us, but we do remember the experiences we had with them and how they affected us.

Unfortunately, some of the negative experiences that students encounter often form their perception of their own abilities and potential. When speaking or engaging with a student, it's imperative to use words that encourage and motivate the student.

I recall a teacher once who was grading a quiz for a student who only earned two correct points out of twenty. The teacher put a +2 on the quiz with a big, smiley face instead of -18 and an F. The student asked the teacher why she graded the quiz that way. She responded enthusiastically, "Because you answered two questions correctly, which means you're on the right track!"

Think back to the teacher in elementary or high school who had the biggest impact on your life. What did that teacher say or do that made such a difference for you? Do you see a student in your current class who reminds you of how you were in school? What would happen if you treated that student the same way your influential teacher treated you when you were in school?

STAYING CHARGED

There will be times when we feel as though we have let ourselves or our students down. It is an inevitable part of life in the classroom. What happens when we feel deflated over a failed lesson? What do we do when we've had a poor performance review because our students just wouldn't settle down that particular day?

My answer would be to seek out the source that best motivates and encourages us. We have options—no matter how tempting it may seem, quitting is not one of them. I encourage you to keep at least a mental list or awareness of the people and resources available to you for support and inspiration.

Here are some things I have found helpful; you may have found others:

Create a file of letters, cards, emails, and pictures from your current or previous students and parents. When you experience a temporary set-back, you can pull out this file and read over the words written by those you have influenced. Remembering the many people whose lives you have impacted is a great encouragement when you are going through a tough time. You can give yourself a motivational pep talk and keep on moving.

Read a book. If you love reading, there is something restorative about immersing yourself in a good book.

Watch an inspirational movie. A story about a struggling student who eventually found success or a teacher who fought through difficult circumstances in order to reach their students can lift your spirits.

14

Listen to music. Listening to music you enjoy has the ability to take your mind off your current issues. Music is also known to activate the pleasure centers of the brain.

Listen to a motivational speech. You can find an infinite variety of talks, speeches, classes, and the like on the Internet, which can help take your mind off a difficult situation and help you to re-establish your focus.

Go outside. Propping your feet up on the back deck or going for a walk might bring you the refreshing you need to start over again the next day.

Get some sleep. Turn off your phone, your tablet and your TV and turn out the lights. Everyone functions better when they are well-rested and not sleep deprived.

Serve others. When you stop focusing on your situation and seek to meet the needs of others, you will almost inevitably leave that experience with the strength you were seeking.

Talk to someone. That person who has always motivated you could be a great source of inspiration in a time when you really need it.

Staying motivated and staying charged have two completely different meanings. Staying motivated comes from an understanding of our intrinsic or extrinsic wiring. This wiring helps us fulfill our work obligations.

Staying charged means staying connected to the source of power inside us. A battery has to hold a charge in order to make a device work; we have to stay charged in order to function, have mental clarity, control our emotions, and physically make it through the day.

All educators understand the period of time between spring break and the last day of school. While we might be striving to work at 100% effort, our energy and physical bodies are usually drained. Our students are bouncing off the walls, state standardized testing is throwing off our schedules, and the thing uppermost in our minds is summer vacation.

As much as we must learn to stay plugged into a source to keep us motivated, we also must learn the value of powering down so we can physically and emotionally recharge. If we keep going at full speed, we will at some point begin to break down.

Think of it in terms of a cell phone. Many cell phones now have apps that help conserve battery life. These apps will reduce the drain of energy on the phone, while still allowing it to function. The less important functions are put on hold so the more vital functions will still have enough power to perform.

Think about the tires on a car. Do you remember how much it cost the last time you had to buy new ones? If we drive over rough ground, hit unseen potholes in the road, or peel away from red lights, the tread on our tires will quickly become dull and the vehicle will soon become unsafe for us to drive. And that's not even considering the cost of yet another set of new tires.

We have to take care of our tires. We have to take care of ourselves. The tires make the car move and we make our classrooms function. If we are not in a good place mentally or emotionally, it can have a negative impact on our students.

I've heard it said that slow and steady wins the race. That saying is especially true when we are up against deadlines and begin to feel insurmountable stress. If we will slow down and power down, we will be better able to assess the situation and strategize a plan. Then we will have the inner resources available to implement that plan and fulfill our mission in the classroom.

It helps to think of education as a marathon, not as a sprint. This means we not only have to be methodical about the well-being of our students for the 180 days we have them, but we must also be methodical about planning for our own well-being. No experienced teacher ever plans to have a science lab, a group presentation, a classroom speaker, a holiday party, and an awards assembly all in the same week. That's a recipe for burnout. Pulling out a yearly calendar and plotting in key dates for projects, major units, field trips and other activities will help us to stay professionally and emotionally balanced.

When we know what motivates us as educators, we will be better able to stay rejuvenated and perform at our very best.

When we understand what motivates our students, we will be better equipped to meet their educational needs.

Understanding how to stay motivated will lay a foundation for developing the plans and procedures, and, most importantly, the vision we want to implement in our classrooms.

FOLLOW-UP QUESTIONS: CHAPTER ONE

1. Are you more intrinsically or extrinsically wired? Or both? What are some examples that illustrate your wiring?

2. How can you communicate positively with students when you see they need encouragement?

3. What are some practical ways you can stay charged during the day, week, month, and even the entire school year?

Chapter Two

When People, Processes, and Procedures Get in the Way

We all have that one friend who tries to tell a joke but can't stop laughing while he tells it. As a result, the joke is no longer funny. Whenever I encounter people like this, I always want to yell, "Stop! You're getting in the way of the joke!" The intention of the person was good—they wanted to cheer me up or give me something to laugh about—but the way in which they were communicating distorted the message. And so, the only person laughing was the one telling the joke.

It is important as educators to make sure that when we are communicating, we are doing so in a way that all parties can accurately interpret and act upon what it is we're saying. Once information has been communicated, it's very challenging to retract mistakes or errors in the content of the message. Being clear and concise in both the written and the spoken word, whether in a large setting or a small setting, makes a difference to the audience. When communication is effective, it establishes trust between the audience and the speaker; or in the case of our classrooms, it establishes trust between students and their teachers.

WHO ARE WE & WHERE ARE WE GOING?

One of the proven ways to promote effective communication within the school is to develop and utilize a mission statement and a vision statement. A mission statement outlines the purpose for the school's existence. It states why they do what they do. A vision statement outlines where the school is headed. It can be thought of as a preview of what the school sees happening in the future.

Having both of these statements will help keep leadership and staff on the same page and allow all parties to continue striving toward the fulfillment of the mission and the vision.

If one person within the organization gets off track, the leadership can redirect that person and keep them in alignment with the stated purposes. When a school does not have a mission statement or a vision statement, it becomes easier for teachers to become discontented with and develop disdain for their leadership.

If we leave for vacation, but refuse to pick a destination or look at a map, how will we know when we have arrived? Having a clear destination and a way to get there will make it much more likely we will arrive at the place where we intended to go.

If our school doesn't have a mission statement or a vision statement, we can ask for the opportunity to meet with the principal and talk about the possibility of creating them. And while we're talking, we can't forget who the statements should center around—our students!

While we should align our teaching goals with the mission statement and vision statement of our school, we can also seek to create our own statements for our individual classrooms.

Guide for Writing and Using a Classroom Mission Statement

- *Write down one-liners describing the purpose of the classroom for that year.*
- *Condense it into a few sentences or a short paragraph.*
- *Include the mission statement in communications with students and parents.*
- *Post it in the front of the classroom.*
- *Recite it from time-to-time with the students.*
- *Include it in the classroom's social media accounts.*

Guide for Writing and Using a Classroom Vision Statement

- *Look ahead to the last day of school.*
- *Draft three or four one-liners describing the goals to be accomplished by then.*
- *Include the vision statement in communications with students and parents.*
- *Post it in the front of the classroom with the mission statement.*
- *Recite it from time-to-time with the students.*
- *Include it in the classroom's social media accounts.*

In the same way we are working each day toward the fulfillment of our academic goals, we must make sure we are living each day in the *mission* statement for our classroom, while working toward the fruition of the *vision* statement. It's important that we model the behavior we want our students to emulate.

We should also integrate elements of our school's statements into our classroom statements. It's important that everyone—from the superintendent or principal all the way down to the students and their parents—is on the same page about their purpose and their future in our classroom.

Organization and structure in our professional lives will help us in more ways than we might realize. A classroom management plan will set expectations for students and help them function successfully within the classroom. The rules and parameters of the school will set expectations for its teachers, which will help them perform successfully within the classroom as well. Some of these expectations might be for the safety of students, others might be for time-savings and cost effectiveness. Some of these expectations might be easy to agree with, while others might mean additional work in the immediate, but greater benefits down the road.

We often look at our classrooms as our domains or our kingdoms. The goal for most us is to make our classrooms student-centered and student friendly. We want our students to walk in on day one and know they are in for the ride of their lives! The organization and policies we put in place even before the students arrive will help make that happen.

We often spend hours and hours each summer on teacher websites. We steal ideas from our teacher friends on social media and work to create new lessons and units. We often thrive on buying an unnecessary amount of index cards and glue sticks; but after all, it's for our students and the atmosphere we are trying to create!

MAKE IT PERSONAL

It is easy to see how our schools and classrooms will benefit from a mission statement and vision statement, but they are equally important in our personal lives. Most of us didn't land in a classroom by mistake. Typically, we have been planning to become educators since middle school or high school and have been dreaming of the day we would be handed the keys to our own classroom.

It is important to stay in alignment with our short-term and long-term goals. When we stay focused, we can see what it is we're doing more clearly. Giving ourselves attainable goals will bring the same sense of accomplishment to our personal lives as it does to our professional lives.

While our personal mission statement can include elements pertaining to our profession, it should also focus on our individual lives. It can be a mantra we can refer to when we get off course or are in the midst of a challenging situation. The aspects of our own lives we include might be relationships with our family and friends, our personal goals—such as running a marathon or saving to purchase a home—or our desires, such as taking a trip to Europe over the summer.

These personal elements do not necessarily have a direct correlation with our professional lives. But because we often feel our profession is our calling, elements of our professional and personal lives can be combined into one statement. Our calling isn't necessarily what we do, but rather who we are. Who we are is always with us, whether we are with our family, our friends, our colleagues, or our students. Our statements can certainly reflect that.

MAGICAL CLASSROOMS

Adopting mission and vision statements in our schools and classrooms helps provide needed structure so that we can accomplish our purposes in the classroom. Following the guidelines of our schools and districts serves a similar purpose.

While we want to build as magical a classroom as we possibly can, there are rules and protocols, whether they are building or district policies, or even policies put in place by the local fire marshal or health department. If our ideas get shut down, we should refrain from complaining. Unless we have attorneys on deck to fight the local fire department on code enforcement because we wanted to hang paper lanterns from the ceiling, we must simply find a different way to display them.

We must also be cognizant of why the processes and procedures were established in the first place and how each particular procedure factors into the big picture.

As an elementary teacher, we might not like the fact that our gym class is at the beginning of the school day. There is only one gym teacher for the 20 teachers in our building. Instead, of filing a complaint with the gym teacher or with our principal, we need to figure out what we can do to best support the schedule. The same applies to other special classes such as art and music.

Even when mistakes are made, we still need to operate in the mindset of what's best for our students. Procedures are in place for a reason, which many times is the safety and well-being of our students and ourselves. If our school has a policy or procedure for field trip forms and we accidentally or inadvertently left information off the form or missed a deadline, we can't blame someone else, the leadership, or the process. We should simply take ownership and meet with the person responsible for processing the forms and see what we can do to fix it. Missing deadlines is never acceptable, especially if we were made aware of the deadline weeks in advance. The only true extenuating circumstance would be something medical or a death in the family, causing us to miss work for weeks at a time. There are an abundance of calendars, reminders, and apps on our phones that we can use to help keep us on track.

THE SENIORS DID WHAT?!

Each year, the seniors at the school in which I serve take a senior trip. The mission of the trip is two-fold: community service and entertainment. While we want the students to learn the value of serving others, we also want them to enjoy their last remaining weeks together as a class. While the location is always a hot-button debate, we are always quick to remind the seniors that it doesn't matter where they go, but it matters who they are with.

We always discuss the code of conduct with the seniors before their trip. There are points on it that are pretty customary for all schools, such as *follow the established handbook policies,* and *respect the chaperoning teachers and parents at all times.* We recently added another point to our code of conduct: *students are not permitted to drive the provided ground transportation.* Now, one might think, "That's a given; of course, a student wouldn't just hop in the rental van and head down the road to McDonald's!"

But much to my dismay and embarrassment, that was added to our code of conduct because a student did exactly that. Student handbooks and faculty handbooks are really just compilations of things the school or district wants done/not done to ensure they stay in compliance. While some points are added proactively, others are added reactively.

DO IT FOR THE STUDENTS

The guidance counselor in my building once moved a student from one high school math teacher to another, based on parent request, but also based on the poor performance and inattentiveness of the student. The original teacher had continuously submitted office referrals for the student and continuously complained about his hyperactivity. When the guidance counselor, acting as an advocate for the student, changed the student's schedule, it upset the original teacher.

The teacher was fuming that he wasn't consulted about the change before it happened. The counselor had simply sent the teacher an email stating that the student was no longer on his roster for 3rd period and had been moved to the other math teacher's class. This was a customary courtesy during the add/drop period during the first few days of school. No ill will was intended.

A few things were evident: the teacher felt that control had been taken from him, and it was evident he hadn't been taking the time to build the necessary relationship with the student. A counselor was simply trying to prevent any further catastrophe by helping get the student into a better learning environment.

We must understand that as professional educators, we have to do what is best for our students, even if this means moving students to different classrooms. We also must respect the decisions made by our peers and leadership. Is it appropriate to ask questions? Absolutely! But we must do so with our egos out of the way. We must do so with what is best for the student at the forefront of the conversation.

What if we have a grand idea that would bring learning to life and revolutionize the way we teach and the way students learn? Ultimately, we have control of how we respond to the parameters we have been given. While we can't control code enforcement, we can control what we do with the information that's been provided to us. More times than not, a district-level policy requires the school board's approval in order to be changed. We have to ask ourselves: Is that one idea worth the added effort?

Instead of becoming frustrated or angry with our leadership, we can seek their guidance for ways that we can still fulfill and accomplish our goals in the classroom. We hold the keys to unlocking student success. Even if we feel like we're continually blocked from teaching with innovation, we can keep moving down our list of ideas until we finally find one that will work. Venting our frustration and expressing our disdain for school policies and procedures with colleagues is never a productive course of action.

MODEL BEHAVIOR

We require our students to follow the rules—teachers must do the same. A few years ago, I began to notice that one particular teacher, whom I will call Mr. Jackson, would be standing at the classroom door greeting students and taking attendance as they entered. The very second the tardy bell rang, he would immediately close the classroom door. Any student who was not already in the room had to get a tardy pass from the office. He did this even if students were within a few feet of the classroom door. These weren't necessarily students misbehaving in the hallway.

I noticed one day that Mr. Jackson left early from the school. Teachers are contractually obligated to remain at the school for one hour after the dismissal bell. Teachers can use this time to prep for the next day, tutor students, or meet with colleagues or parents. I spoke casually with Mr. Jackson the next day and asked him why he had left an hour early the day before. He indicated that he had been going to a medical appointment, which I understood.

I told him that I was becoming increasingly concerned about the number of students who were being marked tardy for his classes. He indicated that these students were late if they weren't seated and ready for class when the tardy bell rang.

I asked him if he thought it was appropriate for teachers to model the behavior that was expected of their students. He agreed that it was, so I asked him a question: "Since you violated an attendance policy for teachers, do you think you should have to endure a consequence?"

He laughed and said, "I get it, Mr. Mills. I will show more grace to students who are eagerly making their way to my classroom. Thank you for being understanding."

CORRECT ANSWER = STUDENTS

When I interview teaching candidates for positions in my building, I always end the interview by asking, "What is the single most important element of a school?" I'm always intrigued by the responses, because they will range from leadership to curriculum to compensation and benefits. I never prompt the interviewee, and I always let them share from their heart. There are no wrong answers, but I think we all would rank our answers differently based on what we perceive to be important and based on our own experiences and expectations.

Secretly and a little selfishly, I'm always looking for candidates to respond by saying, "Students." In my opinion, students are the single most important part of any school. Without students, a school has no reason to exist.

Leadership is paramount. Teachers must have quality curriculum and instruction. Cafeteria food must be hot and cooked thoroughly. The list goes on. But what should be at the center of everything on our list? Students.

I always encourage teachers to look at our students and their families as our customers. We have a product we want them to subscribe to: the education of their child. If we go to the grocery store and ask for help finding the bananas, hopefully a grocery clerk will be courteous enough to direct us to them—or even walk us over to the fruit section. Offering a similar level of courtesy and consideration to our students and their families is imperative.

In my experience interviewing teachers, I have discovered that one of the reasons they leave a school in search of a new one is often as a result of the present leadership. We must work to understand that leaders are people. We have the opportunity to pick our friends, but we often don't have the opportunity to pick our leadership. The average school principal doesn't remain at the same building for 30 years, but there are a lot of teachers who stay in the same school district and even at the same building for 30 years.

Now, imagine how many principals one teacher goes through in a span of 30 years. Let's estimate the number to be six or seven. That's six or seven leadership styles that the staff had to assimilate into their professional experiences. While this is a significant challenge, it is important to keep in mind that even though the leadership changes, the reason for it does not: students.

Our willingness as educators to follow the rules provides a concrete example of the behavior expected of our students, and modeling acceptable behavior is our responsibility.

At the end of the day, let's remember to not let the laughter get in the way of the joke. It takes a tremendous amount of work and effort to provide learning experiences for students that will live on long after they leave our classroom. Let's not let the people, processes, or procedures get in the way of creating a magical and memorable experience for our students.

FOLLOW-UP QUESTIONS:
CHAPTER TWO

1. Do you have a personal mission statement? Do you have a professional mission statement?

2. If yes, are you living by the tenets of your statements?

3. What potential changes do you need to make?

4. If you don't have a mission statement yet, what steps can you take today to begin to develop one?

5. Knowing that you can't necessarily change handbook policies, what are some ways in which you can change your mindset in regard to policies with which you disagree?

Chapter Three

Will Power: Why Not You?

Frozen pizza? That's easy. Meatloaf and mashed potatoes? That's a little more complex! I have a great disdain for cooking. It's not that I'm inept or lack the necessary skills; I just don't have the patience or the energy to figure out ingredients and then use my valuable time to put the meal together.

On the other hand, I do love eating a home-cooked meal. I often find myself eating out three or four nights each week—one or two of them are frequently with my cousin. We enjoy finding new restaurants in the area.

Ashamedly, we once went to a local spot for breakfast and loved it so much that we stayed and ate lunch, too. They even gave us a shout-out on Twitter! We weren't sure if it was a moment to be proud of or if we should've been embarrassed; but nonetheless, we enjoyed the experience and the incredible food.

One night, several years ago, my cousin and I were eating at one of our local pizza joints. I received a call from a telephone number I didn't recognize, even though it was a local number. I often receive calls at random times of the day from students or parents asking questions about homework assignments. Those calls don't bother me—it brings me great joy knowing they care enough to ask questions. However, in this instance, I was too busy consuming pizza and wings to answer my phone. If someone really needed to reach me, they would leave me a message or send me a text.

A few minutes later, my phone rang again, and the same number popped up on the screen. This time, I decided to pick up the phone, and that decision changed my life forever.

"Hello." I said.

I heard a faint voice on the other end of the line: "Mr. Mills, this is Judah."

Judah was a junior, one of the students in my world history class. To put things into perspective, it was November, and Judah had transferred into our school in September. He was a 17-year-old African American, whose biological mother lived locally and whose biological father lived out of state.

Judah said he had just finished with basketball practice and was still at the school waiting for his ride. He had just heard from a relative that his mother was in the hospital again. She had previously battled cancer, while simultaneously undergoing a double hip replacement. He was fearful that her cancer had returned. He indicated that there was some drug use, which upset him, and was one of the main reasons why he had decided to move out of her home.

I quickly finished my meal, parted ways with my cousin, and drove to meet Judah at the school. I knew that I didn't have all the answers for a student going through a situation like his, but what I did know was that I could listen to him and try to be a source of encouragement and strength.

I felt such an overwhelming compassion and empathy for him and knew, from then on, I would do whatever I could to help students like him. While I was talking with him, I saw the toll life was taking on him. He simply didn't have the strength or the experience at his age to maneuver through such difficult circumstances by himself.

I knew that I needed to be a source he could rely on and come to trust. After all, there must have been a reason he chose to call me over all the other adults in his life. There are some students with whom we genuinely connect. It is in those relationships that we can often make the greatest impact, especially when the student holds us in high regard.

Defining Empathy

A few years ago, I was sharing with one of my mentors—who happens to be a leadership development coach—that I understood the situations that students like Judah were going through and knew how they felt. She challenged me by playing devil's advocate about some of the scenarios that I shared with her.

She asked me if I knew what it was like to be an African American youth. She asked me if I knew what it was like to have my father live in a different state and not have a traditional father-son relationship. She asked me if I had the experience of having a mother in the hospital with cancer.

To be honest, I was put off by her questions. I was beginning to realize that even though I have the emotions to feel sad for what a student is going though, there was really no way for me to experience their pain if I were not in their position.

That was when I learned the value of empathy. While having *sympathy* implies that I can feel sorry for someone, having *empathy* means that I can understand the feelings the person is undergoing. On paper, absolutely nothing about Judah's personal life lined up with my experiences, but there was a level of empathy and understanding that created the bud of what would blossom into a relationship that would truly change my life as an educator.

Making a difference for the sake of being recognized or sharing with other people what we've done for students is hollow. There's no substance behind those actions. But when we see a need and gravitate toward it—and it's all we can think about throughout the day— that's a key indicator that we have the answer for that problem. We can't be afraid to take a risk because we never know how that risk will forever change a student's life—and might just change ours in the process.

A few days after I met with him at the school, he asked me if I could take him to the hospital to visit his mother. I stayed in the family waiting room while he visited with her. About thirty minutes into the visit, Judah came down the hospital corridor and into the room where I was sitting. He told me his mother had asked if she could meet me. We met briefly, and I made sure she knew that Judah was in good hands. I told her that I would make sure he was taken care of while she was recovering from her medical setbacks. From that day forward, Judah and I formed a bond which has spanned nearly a decade.

During the rest of his junior and senior years of high school, he slowly worked on rebuilding his relationship with his mother. She was even able to make it to his football senior night, which was a moment he would never forget. It was cold that evening, so we created a warm space for her in the press-box to watch the game.

I made sure that he could eat lunch every day, and that he had a ride home after football and basketball practice. I helped him with his college applications and even drove him to several college football camps. While our respective ages didn't reflect it, our relationship was like father and son. He had a high level of respect for me, and for the decisions I made. He trusted me, and he knew those decisions were made in his best interest. I gave him his space and allowed him to process his emotions, but I didn't allow him to use his situation as an excuse for bad behavior or poor choices. He still had to be held accountable for his actions, as his actions in the present would affect his life in the future.

Judah was strong academically, but had transferred schools several times in high school, which caused some issues with obtaining scholarship offers. He received acceptance letters to well over a dozen colleges and universities across the region. He knew he would either need to get a scholarship or take out tens of thousands of dollars in student loans. Eventually, he was able to put together a scholarship and aid package that would cover the entire balance of his college tuition and board. He was also afforded the opportunity to play college football for a program in West Virginia. I was grateful for that, as I knew this would help keep him focused and accountable while he dealt with the fact that his mother's health was getting progressively worse.

During his sophomore year of college, Judah told me that his mother had been given only a few months to live and was being moved to a hospice facility. Before she entered the facility, she called me. I had not had much interaction with her, nor did I know much about her, other than what Judah had shared with me about her health. She asked if she could meet with me. At this point she was in a wheelchair, but we were able to arrange a meeting at the high school a few days later.

She informed me that she was working on her last will and testament, and that Judah was the executor of her estate. She continued by telling me that she was going to include me in her will as Judah's advisor. In order for him to make any decisions about her affairs, he would have to get my input and approval.

None of my college training had prepared me for a moment like that. One moment I was focused on my students and their standardized test scores; the next moment I was sitting in the school conference room with Judah's mother as she was sharing her situation with me and petitioning me to help her son.

In a condition of bewilderment and confusion, I looked at her and said that I would do anything necessary to help her and Judah during this difficult period. She responded by saying, "He listens to you."

I will never forget her words. While humbling, it reassured me that the effort I was making to help Judah during his high school and college years was worth the time and energy.

Time passed, and Judah would call or text me almost every week with updates on his successes in college. Once, I sent him $70 for a sketch book that he needed for an art class, only to later learn he had earned a C in that course. It's still a touchy subject to this day!

A few months later, I received a call from Judah in my office at the school. He had just heard from his mother's caretaker that he needed to come home right away. I knew this meant his mother had only a few days and possibly only a few hours to live. I told him to meet me at my house and we would drive together to the hospice facility. His younger sisters had left school early and were already in the room with their mother.

Just a few hours later, his mother passed away. Her four children were singing songs of joy, as they knew she was no longer in pain and was now in a happier place. Having never experienced the death of an immediate family member, I found myself at a loss for words.

There was nothing I could say to him that night to alleviate the sadness and grief he was experiencing. As I had done for the few years since that first phone call, I made sure he knew I was available if he wanted to talk.

My intent with Judah was never to replace either of his parents, and it most certainly was not to be written into his mother's last will and testament. I simply saw a need and wanted to help meet that need.

As educators, we might not be the most qualified on paper to meet a certain need, but we might be the most qualified based on our words and actions. If a student has a need, we should strive to meet that need—whether we meet it ourselves or whether we find the right person or group to provide what is needed.

Students respond out of a place of authenticity. They can tell if an adult is genuine or not. For instance, if a student needs paper, give them some paper. While it would be easy to discipline or call the student out publicly for not having all their supplies, a student should be not be afraid to ask for something they need. A student should respond from a place of safety.

Students remember how we treat them and how we make them feel. When they feel that we care for them as a person, they are much more likely to come to us with their issues. They will also respond to us in class with a deeper level of respect.

The power to make a difference in the life of a student starts small. It starts with noticing them. It starts with acknowledging them. It starts with knowing their name. It starts with asking them questions. It starts with simple interaction. This is the real formula for building relationships. The power to make a difference in the life of a student is within our reach. While it might cost us valuable time, energy, or resources, our students need it and deserve it.

FOLLOW-UP QUESTIONS:
CHAPTER THREE

1. How can you show empathy in the classroom in both an emotional way and a practical way while still remaining professional?

2. What needs do your students have that you can help meet?

3. What potential roadblocks are hindering you from engaging with those students?

4. How you can overcome these roadblocks?

Chapter Four

Becoming a Student Again

When I was a fifth grader, I attended an "instrument fitting" night at my middle school. The purpose of the event was to introduce fifth graders to musical instruments and get them excited about the possibility of joining the school band. The band directors knew the value of instilling instrumental music in students at a young age, and they obviously wanted the young musicians to stick with it through high school.

I was instantly drawn to the percussion section. A gentleman from the local music store was demonstrating the portable percussion kits that students could rent and easily transport on the bus and back and forth to school. Once he finished his presentation, the time came for interested students to show that they had the ability and rhythm to play percussion.

Each student had to repeat back a series of hand claps and taps on the piano. The gentleman would play a rhythm, and each student had to replicate it on their own. After a few failed attempts, it was evident that I probably needed to try a different instrument! I had been excited about the possibility of playing the drums, but didn't realize the effort that was necessary to produce a real beat.

I eventually selected the trumpet. I clearly remember playing "Mary Had a Little Lamb" for the first time. While I'm sure my family dreaded listening to me play each night in my bedroom, I was having the time of my life.

I stayed active in band throughout middle school. I had the opportunity to play in a few honors bands and was beyond excited that I was finally getting ready to play in our school's award-winning high school marching band.

As soon as my eighth-grade year wrapped up, we began prepping for high school marching band. I couldn't wait for freshman orientation day. Forty of us marched in the 90-degree heat all day, learned the basics of the program, and of course, had to go through "Freshman Stare Down."

This was a tradition and rite of passage at our school. The freshmen had to line up and stand at attention while the seniors did everything they could to make them laugh. If anyone laughed, they had to run laps until the last freshman finally broke rank and laughed.

The first football Friday of the school year finally arrived, and I couldn't wait to march down the field that evening in both the pre-game and half-time performances. I got off the school bus around 3:00 p.m., prepped my uniform and polished my trumpet. I couldn't wait for my mom to get off work so she could drive me back to the school by 6:00 p.m. when the band room opened.

As was the custom, band members arrived at the school wearing t-shirts and shorts, then changed into their full uniforms closer to the field report time of 7:00 p.m. There were 125 of us in the band, and the excitement was electric in the band room that day.

It was nearly 6:30 p.m., and students were starting to get dressed. I opened my garment bag, pulled out the hanger that held my uniform, and threw it over the back of a chair. I reached for my black socks, white shoes, and my hat and plume, setting everything out. I picked up my uniform and unzipped the jacket. My heart sank and panic set in—my pants were missing! There was no way I could march without them. I did not want to miss my very first opportunity to march in the high school band!

I looked in the garment bag, my book bag, all around the band room, and even in the parking lot, but my pants were nowhere to be found. I called my mom from the director's office and told her my horror story. Even though we lived about twelve minutes from the school, she somehow found my pants and dropped them off to me within 6 minutes! My first band experience had a lot more drama than I had anticipated, but my super-mom saved the day!

I say all this because no matter our age or level of experience, there will always be firsts and first days of school for us. It's important that we prepare and develop ourselves and our routines so that we can become effective in our performance as educators. We will inevitably make mistakes or embarrass ourselves in front of our students. When we do, we can look for the humor in the situation; but more importantly, we can look for the learning moment within the mistake.

It is easy to see the humor in my first band experience now—it was not so easy then. I had not yet developed a routine of double-checking everything myself, but I soon did. I definitely did not want a repeat performance like that! I didn't know it at the time, but it was one of my first introductions to the value of professional development.

If we were to take an inventory of how many professional development sessions and workshops we've had to endure, I'm sure the number would be astounding, depending on how many years we've worked as educators.

When my attendance is required at yet another workshop, I often dread the thought of listening to another speaker ramble about a topic that probably doesn't even interest me. If we had to list every professional development experience we've participated in and write a one-sentence description on how each one changed our life, could we do it?

Hear me out: I firmly believe in professional development for educators. There are times as a building principal that I see areas for improvement that could apply to more than one teacher or department. It becomes my responsibility as the instructional leader of my building to figure out strategies that will help to develop all the parties involved.

The quickest way to disseminate this type of information is typically through workshops and meetings that require the entire staff to be in attendance. Depending on the time of day or type of day, sometimes these meetings are beneficial and sometimes they just simply aren't. We all know that in August, we're fired up and refreshed, and we have a renewed sense of purpose. We also know that scheduling a professional development workshop at the end of the school day in April is probably not going to yield the same results.

CALCULATING RATIOS—30:1 OR 1:30

Not only should we always be learning and growing in our content area, but we should also be growing in our professional paths. We must set the example and set the standard for our students. I once heard an educator state upon retirement, "I didn't teach one year thirty times, I taught for thirty different years." Her statement indicated that she not only took into account the unique sets of students she taught each year, but she also made sure that her instruction was relevant, it was updated, and it accommodated the needs of the learners.

We can't become relevant and learn about what's new in education by reading our old college textbooks. We need to engage ourselves in what is happening on social media and in the world beyond our school building and our immediate sphere of influence.

There are many ways to grow as an educator. I've gleaned a wealth of information by participating in chats on Twitter with other educators who share similar passions to grow in their professional journeys.

We have to be confident enough to know in what areas we need growth. Once we have identified these areas for improvement, we should seek out the appropriate experts or leading authorities on the subjects and begin to grow our understanding. We need to seek ways to implement and apply what we've learned, all while keeping our students as the center focus.

We often forget that we can turn to our students and look to them as teachers. Our students have the ability to teach us more than we could possibly teach them. This is accomplished by both observing our students and by interacting with them. Observation is a great teacher—if you've ever sat on a bench at your local mall or department store and watched people, you know that you can learn a lot by simply observing. Sometimes it turns into a quite a fashion show—you learn what to wear and what not to wear!

We can also learn by interacting. Have you ever received a text message and interpreted it one way, only to learn later that the message was intended to mean something totally different? When we interact with our students, we have the opportunity to learn first-hand what it is they mean and what it is they need.

We should steer away from labeling students, especially if we haven't taken the time to learn more about them. Labels are limiting. We should want more *for* our students and more *out of* our students. They deserve to be held to a higher standard than what our patience or apathy might want.

MATURATION MOMENTS: STARTING OVER

I know the excitement that comes with receiving the roster of students for the new school year, but here is a challenge: refrain from reviewing their behavior record from the previous year. All students deserve a fresh start. When someone we are around every day starts to lose weight, it may take us a while to notice. However, if we run into someone we haven't seen in six months and they've lost 30 pounds, it's really easy to recognize it.

Students are the same way. A lot of change can take place between June, July, and August, and we should give the student the benefit of the doubt that they have matured and are ready to conquer a new grade level.

We should also remember to be curious. We might be experts in our content area or grade level, but we are not experts in the individual people our students are. We should seek to learn *why* our students think the way they do. Each of our students should be treated differently, based on what their needs and learning styles require.

We often leave out the demographic of the student, yet that key information can sometimes make all the difference in student learning. A student's political and spiritual viewpoint is often influenced by their parents, family, or community. We shouldn't try to change their viewpoint or stance on issues, but we should try to understand their ideas. Understanding their experiences and backgrounds is crucial.

Teachers should also practice the art of patience. Yelling at students because they aren't grasping a concept as fast as we would like is simply inexcusable. Rushing a student through an authentic learning experience because it's time to transition to the next lesson isn't fair to the student. Using anger or frustration instead of words to communicate with students has detrimental effects. It drastically alters the capacity of that student to trust a teacher.

When we are intentional with our lesson planning and strive to create experiences for our students, our students will almost certainly create an experience that will change us. We often don't set out to create experiences that will change our lives, but we often end up with that result when we are methodical about providing a quality and engaging learning experience for our students.

Think back to when you were in high school or college and you worked especially hard on a project or assignment. Did you ever receive your score back only to see that it was lower than you felt you deserved? Or think about your most recent teaching evaluation. Did you receive feedback from your principal that you felt was harsh or wasn't indicative of your teaching abilities in the classroom?

These situations can be challenging. I am probably not the only one who has typed an email response out of anger, deleted it, retyped it, then deleted it again, only to type it a third time and leave it in my drafts overnight. We should guard against responding out of anger; we should wait until we can respond from a position of understanding.

Every principal or instructional leader has their own scope of experience. When we undergo an evaluation, our teaching methods, our classroom management, and our technology integration are being evaluated based on the evaluator's level of experience. Their feedback doesn't make what we do in the classroom wrong, but it does give us a different perspective. Just like we want our students to receive our feedback as constructive, we must be mature enough to do the same. When we are willing to become a student in every situation, we will be better equipped with the resources we need to help our students.

Professional development is a continual process. It is up to us to make the most of the opportunities that come our way, whether they are in a workshop, from an evaluation, or learned along the way.

Creating experiences for our students that will empower them to become successful and productive both in our classrooms and beyond should be at the core of each decision we make and every conversation we have regarding our professional development. As *we* grow and develop, so will our students.

FOLLOW-UP QUESTIONS: CHAPTER FOUR

1. In what ways can you accomplish professional development outside of the school?

2. How can you integrate social media into your professional learning community?

3. Knowing that labels are limiting, what are a few ways in which you can change your mindset in order to provide students with the opportunity to grow and mature past their previous mistakes?

Chapter Five

Pouring from an Empty Cup

I was watching American Idol recently and the participants who had advanced to the Hollywood round were performing for the judges. For this particular episode, the remaining contestants were paired up and had only one day to learn a duet, complete with the accompaniment, and perform it live on television. I could almost sense the stress and tension that the contestants were going through as I watched the show. Most of them stayed up for the duration of the night rehearsing their parts.

Two contestants took the stage and the music began to play. The first person in the duet began to sing, and then the camera panned to the second person, who had a look of sheer panic on her face. She was humming along with the music, but she had forgotten the lyrics to the song!

Imagine how she felt—she had met her duet partner yesterday and learned a new song overnight, only to forget the words on live television. The pressure had gotten to her, and she wasn't able to perform to the same level she had during rehearsal just hours before.

SANDCASTLES ON THE BEACH

I feel as though this is what state standardized testing often does. We spend so much of our time in the classroom preparing and overpreparing our students for standardized tests, that sometimes I think we psych our students out and they aren't able to adequately transfer the knowledge they've learned onto the test. For schools that are data-driven, this often affects both their statistics and their instructional approach with students. I won't get into the debate of whether or not teachers should be held accountable for their students' state test scores, but I would like to go on record and say that an effective teacher will ensure that their students are prepared.

Teaching is like continually pouring knowledge into a cup and slowly filling it up—lesson after lesson, project after project, test after test—so that our students can find success. The real prize is when the test results come back, and we learn that our students scored well.

While schools and districts often thrive on performance measures such as high standardized test scores, there should be no competition when it comes to education. We should seek differentiated success for each student. When our instruction for each student is intentional and our students are mastering the content, we are then pouring out of our cup of knowledge and sharing it with them. This can give us a sense of satisfaction that can't be manufactured; it must be experienced.

Or, we can think of it this way: when we build a sandcastle at the beach, we first have to pack sand tightly into a bucket until it's full, put the bucket of sand where we want it, flip the bucket over, and pull the bucket off the sand. We follow this same pattern over and over until our sandcastle is complete.

When we enter the classroom on the first day of school, our students are like those empty buckets. It becomes our mission to fill each one with the knowledge they individually need, to the point where they can demonstrate what it is that they've learned. We must meet students where they are, not *where we think they should be.*

Let's say we are teaching 7th grade mathematics. If we discover, based on the results of our pre-assessment on the first week of school, that one of our students is clearly testing at a 5th grade level, we obviously have to create a plan to help close the achievement gap. If we begin teaching that student at the 7th grade level, there will inevitably be information that they haven't mastered, creating a divide from what they know versus *what we think they should know.*

We can liken this to a cup filled with ice. The ice represents what the student knows. However, to fill the cup completely, we have to add liquid. In this case, let's use water. Once we've added the water, which represents our instruction, the water fills up the space in and around the ice and brings wholeness to the picture. The water closes the achievement gap, so to speak, allowing the student to fully comprehend our instruction.

In all this, we must remember to treat students fairly. This doesn't apply only to classroom rules and procedures, but to instruction as well. Not every student performs at the same level academically. For some, schoolwork is easy. For others, schoolwork might be a challenge and require twice as much time. However, both students might earn the same grade. We should never assume that just because a student earned a high mark it did not require effort.

When we meet students at their level, and when we treat them fairly and with dignity, we are creating more of a relationship with them than we realize. Students notice when other students receive special treatment or privileges. It creates envy, which is not a healthy feeling, especially if a student receives special opportunities because they finished their work early or earned a higher grade. A divide between "smart" and "non-smart" students is more easily recognized among the students themselves than we sometimes realize.

HOLISTIC EDUCATION: EXPLORE & ESTABLISH

In a holistic approach, we should consider the full, or whole, well-being of the student. Think of it like the human body. For the body to function at its full capacity, all of the parts have to work together. For instance, while I use my whole hand to pick up a glass, it is the combination of muscles, bones, and ligaments within my hand that makes that task possible.

When a student comes to class without their homework completed, it's imperative that we explore

56

why before we too hastily assign a zero and assume the worst. In order to get to the root of an issue, especially if a relationship hasn't yet been established with the student, beginning with a private conversation from a position of concern will likely yield much better results than an automatic zero.

Sometimes, even a phone call home to a parent letting them know we are concerned about missing homework will have a positive impact on the student, letting the student know we care. Students rarely want to disappoint the people in their lives who care about their well-being and success. This applies equally to other situations such as students who might be hungry, students who sleep in class, or even students acting out of their normal character.

Another part of exploring who our students are involves learning about their interests and then figuring out when and where we can integrate those interests into either our instruction or our interactions with them. We can learn who their favorite musicians are and what their favorite songs are. We can get to know their favorite sports teams, superstar athletes, video games, authors, and the list goes on.

At the same time, it's good for students to see our human side. We can share our interests and hobbies with them, too. When they share their favorites, we can take the opportunity to ask them if they've heard of our favorites. This creates the opening for dialogue. We can be creative by pulling up a YouTube video or playing a song from iTunes. There is great benefit in creating a "Mom, you'll never believe what Mr. Smith did in class today" moment when we implement these elements into our lessons. Students rarely will forget an experience.

After we've explored, we should then seek to establish. When we establish trust, we establish relationship. It is never acceptable to mistreat a student by holding their *present* hostage to their *past* mistakes.

I recall an incident where a teacher became frustrated with a rather hyper student. She attempted to gain his attention by bringing up an incident that occurred earlier that year in the classroom. She was trying to help him realize that his actions were going to lead to an unwanted consequence—another out-of-school suspension. This particular student didn't respond well to the comments, and the incident escalated to the point that the administration and parents became involved.

The student noted in his written statement that while he knew he didn't respond to the teacher in a respectful manner, he also didn't think it was professional of the teacher to bring up his previous behavior incident. He felt as though he was being labeled, and that regardless of what he did, he was going to be thought of as "the bad kid." This scenario doesn't help establish trust.

There is benefit in learning from the past in order to help a student. If we had a student who was struggling academically, we would be expected to review the academic record of that student. Meeting with parents, emailing the former principal or teacher, or meeting with the guidance counselor could all yield beneficial results for both us and the student. If we do choose to review the behavior records of our students, my plea is that we do not hold the student accountable for the previous year.

Just imagine that we had a very unsatisfactory year teaching in the classroom. Would we want that year to be brought up in the middle of a future interview, contract negotiation, or classroom observation review? Wouldn't we want to start with a clean slate?

I've been in staff meetings where we talked about how to best help a struggling student, whether it pertained to academics or behavior. The room would typically be split right down the middle in these types of discussions. There was always a group of teachers who had never had academic or behavioral problems with the student, but there was always another group of teachers who had encountered struggle after struggle with the exact same student.

What I've noticed in the latter is that either the student was not being sufficiently challenged or the teacher hadn't built a level of trust with the student, and hadn't established a relationship with him. My biggest cringe moment is when a teacher tells me, "I talked with other teachers, and he's giving them issues, too, with his behavior."

That tells me that very little effort was expended in finding solutions for the student. I would much rather hear, "I asked a few other teachers for ideas on how I can best meet his needs."

DON'T SUFFER IN SILENCE

In order to pour out of our cup and into the lives of our students, our cup must be full. We can't pour out of an empty cup. This means we must take the necessary steps both professionally and personally to ensure we have what our students need. I wish I had the magic solution for teacher observations, because it almost always seems that students are perfectly behaved if an administrator is in the classroom. At the same time, the teacher spends several extra hours of planning time preparing a lesson to "wow" the observer during the observation. Is it just me, or does something about this entire system seem off?

For most administrators, it's easy to pinpoint areas of growth opportunity for teachers when they are evident. For example, from my experience, when students and parents are calling or emailing repetitively, I know it's time for a review of practices or procedures pertaining to that teacher.

Sometimes, it's not as easy to figure out areas of growth opportunity if an area isn't immediately noticeable or if it is not being addressed by the teacher. The average teacher isn't going to go to their boss and say, "I struggle in this area!" We usually find ways, whether through the help of colleagues or via the Internet, to try and figure out solutions to our problems before they escalate to the building principal.

We might be dynamic teachers. We might come to school daily prepared with superb lessons that engage and motivate our students to achieve mastery. We

60

might plan the most exciting field trips and use the most creative reward and incentive programs in the building. But we might struggle with parent communication; parents might intimidate us. We might have had one bad experience during our first year of teaching, and now we are hesitant to reach out to the parents with whom we need to communicate. This is a prime example of a weakness that might not be noticeable to the naked eye, but one for which we know we need help in order to mature or grow. We might receive stellar scores across the board on our annual observation, but we might also be suffering in silence.

When I hire new teachers, I try to spend some time before the school year starts by getting to know them as people, not just as professionals. I took a new teacher to lunch recently, and on our way back to the school, I asked him, "Ok, now that you've been hired, what areas do you really need my help in?"

We all know that when we're asked the dreaded question in an interview—*Can you tell me three of your strengths and one of your weaknesses?*—we always pick a weakness that isn't too weak but is still acceptable.

After my question, I was pleasantly surprised at the direction the conversation with the new teacher went, and I was able to provide some coaching and professional development opportunities for him as a new teacher both in the field and in our building. Because there was a level of trust established, a relationship was formed. The new teacher knew that I had his best interest at heart and that I wanted him to perform at his best for our students.

Now, he's been able to freely come to me with issues, and vice versa. Our ability to communicate openly and honestly is due to the relationship that was established—rooted in integrity and pure motive at the onset. It has proven to be very productive. As a young teacher, he has a very well-managed classroom and brings his best to the classroom every day. He knows I have his back, and he in turn wants to make sure he does the same for his students.

Even though there are scheduled professional development days at our school and in our district, we should seek ways in which we can grow and develop outside of what is required. Most schools and districts will pay the registration fees for seminars and workshops—if we simply ask.

There are numerous ways we can seek, and find, personal or professional growth. We can take some time during our planning period and observe our colleagues in action. We can stop by our local bookstore and find some reading material that covers a topic in which we're seeking growth. We can ask a mentor for guidance and coaching. We can also be transparent with them and have them observe us in our craft.

We should also take care of ourselves personally. We cannot pour out of an empty cup, so staying connected to a source that keeps us motivated and that keeps our cup full is important. It is never acceptable to sacrifice our own welfare or health at the expense of our students. We should know our breaking point. We should know when enough is enough. We must keep ourselves accountable and know when it's time to slow down and refill.

I always love August and September because teachers are coming back to the school with their cups filled to the brim. The word *no* is rarely, if ever, found in their vocabulary, and they often feel like they can run through a troop and leap over a wall. They feel limitless!

As the year progresses, I believe it's perfectly normal for that energy to slowly drain. Sometimes, we get stuck in the middle of the proverbial rat race and weeks pass by before we even realize it. Our excitement and zeal slowly turn into worksheets and silent sustained reading assignments. Our intent to help students with project-based learning turns into just telling our students to research on their Chromebooks during class. A little part of us gets excited when we know there is going to be an assembly, especially when it's during the period with our "challenging" students! Some of this stems from not taking the time to ensure our cups are full. We must be intentional about our day, every day.

It bears repeating: our students deserve our absolute best each and every day. If we want to see the results we desire or build the relationships we want, we must be willing to go above and beyond the template of classroom management to meet the needs of our students. We must seek ways in which we can grow professionally and protect ourselves personally in the process. Once we've accomplished this, our cups will truly be overflowing.

FOLLOW-UP QUESTIONS:
CHAPTER FIVE

1. How can you prepare students for assessments without distressing them unnecessarily?

2. How can you re-evaluate your methods to make sure students are treated fairly?

3. How can you create a "Mom, you'll never believe what Mr. Smith did in class today!" moment?

4. What are some practical ways that you can refill your "cup"?

Chapter Six

Teaching vs. Learning

Be honest—have you ever judged a book by its cover? While it's obvious that the content of the book is what really matters, for some reason, I'm always drawn to books that have intriguing covers. I also find it mundane when the author's face is plastered on the front cover because that doesn't tell me anything about what I should expect to read. I'm always looking for something different and unique that draws me in.

Or, what about a television series? I've often found myself starting a series on Netflix that might have three or four seasons, and within the first few episodes, I start to second guess why I thought the show would be entertaining to watch. However, there have been those other times when I've become engrossed in the show and suddenly realize five hours have passed and I've watched an entire season.

We have all had those moments in life—whether from the choice we made to read a certain book or watch a certain show—that potentially have a much larger meaning. I had a moment like that, which changed how I view those in my profession.

At the end of each school year, we have a tradition where we provide our graduating seniors with the opportunity to share parting words of wisdom to the underclassmen in a school-wide assembly. I believe there is great benefit in having all grade levels in attendance, not just the rising seniors.

The seniors will often give "shout-outs" to teachers, thanking them for the investment that was made in their success as students. The student council officers always present small gifts and tokens of appreciation to the seniors, too. We invite parents and relatives, as this is the last hurrah before the graduation ceremony later that week.

One year, a senior was sharing words of encouragement with the student body and closed by thanking several teachers. Directing her comments toward one particular teacher, she said, "I wish to thank Mr. Jackson for not just being a teacher, but for being an educator."

I've never forgotten the impact of the words. It was one of those *"What did she just say?"* moments. From that day to the present, I am continually analyzing what it takes to move from the initial act of teaching into the process of educating.

I came to the realization that no matter which side of the line someone might fall on, both teaching and educating are extremely hard work. It is not an easy feat working with students and seeking ways in which to inspire and motivate them each and every day. As I sought out the differences, there were a number of things I realized.

EDUCATING BEGINS WITH TEACHING

Teaching is focused on the curriculum and the mechanics of teaching a lesson. Teaching ensures that objectives align with the state academic content standards. An interactive lesson might include an array of methodologies and approaches, such as direct instruction, group discussion, pair-and-share, and even the use of Chromebooks, cell phones, and other technologies. A lesson taught almost always ends with a homework assignment that helps the student practice more of what they learned that day.

Educating is focused on the student. Educating moves beyond the basic components of teaching a lesson and focuses on the progress and the development of the student. Educating is a process that uses teaching not just to accomplish what's written in a lesson plan, but to instruct students in such a way that there is evidence that learning has occurred.

If we aren't tactical and intentional about what we are teaching—making sure that we take time to gauge student learning—then we are simply wasting our time. More importantly, we are wasting the time of our students. We all know that classroom time is precious, especially when we have to plan around the inevitable interruptions: fire drills, snow days, gym class, assemblies, and the list goes on.

Educating students focuses on their general well-being, making sure that their physiological needs are met before moving into teaching. When these needs are met, the student is then prepared for learning. Examples of meeting physiological needs include making sure students have clean clothes and appropriate hygiene items, figuring out how to provide lunch for students in need, asking a student about the condition of their sick parent, or asking what can be done to help them through a tough time.

LESSON TAUGHT, LESSON LEARNED?

Do you look forward to staff potlucks because you know one of your co-workers makes the best chocolate chip cookies that you've ever tasted? I'm always amazed at the way chocolate chip cookies can contain the same basic ingredients but taste so vastly different. Even if we buy our cookies from the grocery store, we will have a preference based on taste.

Even though the cookies have the same ingredients, it's often the quantity or quality of the ingredients that makes all the difference. It might be the order in which ingredients were added to the mixing bowl or the amount of certain ingredients used that can drastically change the taste of the cookie.

One decision can be transformative for our students. Just because we teach a lesson, it doesn't mean that our students learned the lesson. There are strategies put into place that help serve as a system of checks and balances in our instruction that help us yield the greatest results.

Implementing pre-assessments, quizzes, post-assessments, and other forms of homework and assignments allows us to see whether or not our students have learned what it is we've taught. It's imperative that we use these metrics, as the ultimate measure of success for our students is going to be how well they comprehended what we prepared for them.

I ask teaching candidates in their interview the following question: "If more than half of your class fails a test or assignment, who should take the blame?"

The candidate will pause, and then say something very diplomatic such as, "I would take the blame, and I would take the responsibility of reteaching the lesson or finding a different way to measure student success."

Don't get me wrong—there are other factors that are often at play, such as the demographic of your students, whether or not the class just came back from physical education, or whether they were getting ready to head to lunch.

I believe that most students want to perform well, but we have to remember that there are only a certain number of hours in a day, and our students have to prioritize their days, too. For some, survival might be their only focus while at school, not studying.

TALK IT OUT

It is particularly challenging to put our agendas aside for the betterment of a student. I have a policy at my school which specifies that if I receive an office referral from a teacher, the decision as to the next level of consequence rests with me, and the teacher can't be upset about the outcome. This has encouraged teachers to deal with issues inside their own classrooms, rather than refer them to me.

Many issues involving students, whether behavioral or academic, can be resolved by having a simple conversation. Of course, I understand that there are certainly instances where procedural discipline is necessary based on the violation of handbook policies.

There have been times when I will conference with a student and then send the student back to class within the same period. I know the internal feeling that often rises up when we believe the student should have been suspended or received a harsher consequence.

When student discipline issues rise to the level of the school administration, it's imperative that decisions are made that will best meet the needs of the student. In these situations, my goal as a principal isn't just to "teach them a lesson." Chances are we've forgotten hundreds of such "lessons" we've been taught over the years. My purpose is to ensure that students learn how to redirect or rechannel their energy or behavior in a way that allows them to achieve their goals and helps them find success at school.

HELLO, MY NAME IS...

To best meet the needs of the learners in our classrooms, we have to know our learners. Educators accomplish this in various ways. Some teachers distribute questionnaires at the start of the school year which include questions that will help them better help the student.

For instance, it might include questions such as: *Do you prefer to answer questions aloud or by writing them down? Do you like to speak in front of your peers? Do you learn better by working alone or in a group?* These types of questions prompt students to think about their learning style and preference and provide teachers with valuable information about the student.

When building rapport with students, we need to make sure the flow of information goes both directions. This ensures that the students know our procedures and policies, and are integrated into our classroom rules and expectations.

I've also heard of teachers having 15-minute interviews with each student in the class. This might work better for elementary or middle school teachers who have one group of 20 students versus a high school teacher who has been assigned over 100 students each school day. This approach helps the teacher hear directly from the student, and it helps create a level of trust.

All students want to be noticed. We spend a lot of time dealing with the students who have discipline issues or with the ones who can't seem to sit still, but the quiet students also want and deserve to be recognized for the work that they do in the classroom, too. If we think about it, they are the ones who are making our lives easier.

When I was teaching high school social studies, I contacted three parents every Friday and shared something positive about their student with them. Often, it was something as simple as telling them that their student had earned an "A" on a test that week, or that their student had consistently come to class all year prepared. On other occasions, it might have been to tell them how much I appreciated their student's cooperative and attentive attitude, and that I recognized that it stemmed from great parental support.

One of the parents I called had a son with a reputation for being written up by other teachers in the building. When the mother saw it was the school calling, she answered the phone by asking, "What did he do now?"

Thankfully, she was ecstatic when I told her I was just calling to tell her that her child had earned one of the highest scores on a quiz that day. From this, I gained a level of trust with that parent which helped down the road when I did have to contact her regarding her son's frequent outbursts in class. She supported me 100%, and with our partnership, we began to see significant improvement in his behavior.

In order to break that plane from teaching to learning, it's imperative that we really know our students. I often tell the teachers in my building that even though they have three sections of sophomore English, just because a lesson worked for one section, doesn't mean the same lesson will work for the next group. This is true differentiated instruction. When we assess what students need, regardless of whether or not we take a traditional path, we are meeting their needs. It doesn't matter which route we take, as long as all of our students end up in the same location.

The hardest part about differentiated instruction is getting students and parents on board. While we might have an academic success plan for each student, our students only see what's directly in front of them. If they perceive that another student or group has an easier or less challenging homework assignment, they will inevitably complain or inquire as to the fairness of the assignment. We have to keep in mind that what *is* fair is that each student has the opportunity to receive an education. What *isn't* fair is for the educator not to meet the student's need.

Let's work to change dinner table conversations across the nation. When our parents asked us what we learned in school that day, we probably answered, "Nothing." Am I right?

Let's set the bar high and challenge our students, when they are asked that question, to unload the lessons of the day on their parents. I believe parents will be more apt to partner with us and trust us as educators when they believe that their children are being challenged and are actually learning.

FOLLOW-UP QUESTIONS:
CHAPTER SIX

1. How can you move from teaching to educating in your classroom?

2. How can you better redirect student behavior in order to meet the needs of your students?

3. What are practical ways that you can get to know your students individually?

Chapter Seven

Shorts in the Circuit to Success

I recently purchased a new home. I found out that there are some things they don't tell you when you buy your first house! Boxes don't unpack themselves; walls don't paint themselves; grass doesn't cut itself. Someone (in this case, me!) has to apply some effort to make these things happen.

When I moved into the home, it was late September. I was excited to begin painting, making the space my own. At the same time, I was busy working at the school, especially staying late for fall sports. I would come home exhausted, but still try to spend some time unpacking and making a home out of my house. The condition of the yard was the last thing on my mind.

I was leaving the house early in the morning before the sun came up and, most days, coming home after the sun went down. Who would even notice how tall my grass was getting? Secretly, though, I worried that my neighbors were judging me, because they spent a lot of hours in their well-taken-care-of yards.

With only a few weeks left in the traditional mowing season in Ohio, I decided to tackle the grass. Thankfully, the old homeowners had left me their gently used riding lawnmower!

I made my way to the shed and started up the mower. I spent the next hour mowing my half acre lot. When I was done, I parked the mower back in the shed, walked to the garage, jumped in my car, and headed down the road for a quick dinner at a restaurant in town. I was too exhausted to even attempt to make dinner.

As I drove back up to my house after dinner, I noticed how terrible my yard looked. I hadn't noticed it when I was in the middle of mowing, but the grass had grown so tall that, as I mowed, it left large piles of clippings scattered all throughout the yard.

My momentum was shot at that point. I was working so diligently at taking care of what needed to be done, only to look back and realize that this was an interruption to my success. I knew that I eventually had to get back out in the yard and rake up the debris or this would continue to be an issue every time I mowed. I wished it would just disappear—but ignoring the work that needed to be done in my yard wasn't going to make it go away.

SCIENCE LESSON: ELECTRICAL CURRENT

When electrical current is flowing and there is an interruption, it's referred to as a short. This occurs when a circuit has little or no resistance. When there is no resistance, the flow of the current can become dangerously high. If the current is flowing through a wire, it can heat up the wire and even cause a fire.

There are elements that can be included in a circuit to help prevent overheating, such as a fuse. A fuse is designed to protect the circuit from reaching a dangerously high level of current. In addition, a fuse is designed as a built-in mechanism that once the current reaches a certain level, it automatically shuts off the circuit, preventing any potential or further issues.

Seeing all the grass clippings in my yard after I mowed were like a short in a circuit. The grass clippings laying everywhere prevented me from seeing my overall success with the condition of my yard. Taking the time to rake the excess yard waste from the yard acted as a fuse or circuit breaker, allowing for future mowing to go smoothly and without issues.

JAYLEN'S STORY

I'm reminded of a student that I had in class several years ago named Jaylen. Frankly, he was dealt a rather challenging hand in life. He found out at the age of 16 that he had been adopted. He had noticed in a picture that the name on the hospital wristband of the woman holding him when he was an infant didn't match his mother's name. This discovery angered him. He could never understand why he had not been told.

I taught him as a freshman, and he was a genuinely intelligent student. His adoptive parents were very involved in his life, and his entire family was active in their local church. His parents participated in the church choir, and he played the organ. They cared enough for his life that they made sure he was in a position to receive a quality education. He was a great football player and had the potential to achieve greatness in high school and beyond.

However, Jaylen's decisions slowly led him down a path of drugs and gang affiliation. One of the influences in his life was a relative whom he admired and respected as a role model, but who was in prison. Jaylen had been attending a private school, but he was forced to withdraw due to drug use.

He returned to the school in which I was working when he was a senior. He needed eight credits to graduate that following spring. He had exactly eight classes in an eight-period day, so he knew that he needed to pass every single class in order to participate in the commencement ceremony and receive his high school diploma. The pressure was on!

At the semester change, it was evident that Jaylen was significantly farther behind than he realized. Four of his classes were in our online program. A student had the entire year to complete each class, but if they had not achieved at least half of the curriculum by Christmas break, it would become mathematically impossible to finish the assignments before the end of the school year.

His attendance became increasingly worse. He would attend school just enough to keep the school from legally having to report him as truant. The days he did show up, he often showed up late. I suppose at that point, we were just happy he was physically in the building, so we didn't bring up the fact that he was late. I was able to build rapport with him, and I knew that if

I continually harped on him about his attendance, he would stop showing up all together.

We had a challenging conversation with Jaylen, and we stressed the urgency of him coming to school to complete his assignments. We set up after school hours for him to stay and get caught up, but he didn't take advantage of the opportunity. His parents wanted the best for him; but by this time, he had turned 18 and hit the streets, very rarely returning home.

As graduation drew closer and closer, Jaylen began to feel the pressure. He decided that he didn't want the stress of trying to get everything finished, especially if the possibility existed that he wouldn't meet the deadline. In his eyes, it was a gamble he wasn't willing to take. After discussions with the school administration, he made the decision to withdraw the week before what would've been his high school graduation.

The phrase *"you can lead a horse to water, but you can't make him drink"* is cliché and overused, but nevertheless applicable in so many ways in education. We have all had students whom we wanted to help become successful, but who would simply not put forth the effort, or could not see the benefit in doing so. The worst feeling is when you know that even though a student is extremely intelligent or gifted, they are not performing at the level you know is attainable for them.

It saddens me when a student is testing at the honors or accelerated level, yet they want to take the non-honors or non-accelerated courses. I often hear, "It helps my GPA." But so does taking an honors course and scoring well, and so does being challenged with content that is more appropriate for your academic ability level.

In the situation with Jaylen, so many teachers and staff members wanted success for him because he was fully capable. But because he was so engaged in his new-found "street" life, he was more focused on his literal survival than he was on his academic survival. While some teachers perceived him as disrespectful, he just forgot to shut off "street" mode when he came into the school. Based on my experiences with him, he was—and still is—a great kid.

As in the circuitry reference, our students often consider us the "resistance." They also often forget that resistance is necessary in order for a circuit not to short out. They don't always realize how much we want them to succeed, or how much we don't want them to crash and burn.

Jaylen looked at the magnitude of work in front of him and realized that it was too overwhelming for him, and he was hesitant to try to complete it. I think in this case, the school also acted much like a fuse, trying to slow him down, get him focused, and keep him on the right path before something tragic happened to him as a result of his poor decisions, especially always being "on the go" in the streets without any structure or accountability. We were trying to protect the circuit so it wouldn't go into overload.

His personal life could have been a lot worse had it not been for teachers and coaches staying on top of him and calling him when he wasn't present at school. Many times, he simply said he couldn't come, but at least we knew he was still alive. That built-in level of semi-accountability made him realize that we were still on his team.

Fast forward. Nearly two years later, I received a text message from Jaylen's parents asking if I would be willing to forward them a copy of his transcript. I responded immediately, and told them I would take care of the transcript under one condition: Jaylen had to call me and update me on his life.

I had spent the last 12 months trying to track Jaylen down, but with no success. I would never tell him this, but I even looked online at the jail bookings one day when I discovered that his phone line had been disconnected. I assumed the worst, but I remained vigilant in my attempts to reconnect with him.

About fifteen minutes after I responded to that text, my phone rang, and it was Jaylen. I felt a sense of relief to finally have made contact with him again. He began by telling me that he was embarrassed about the condition of his life and that he had wanted to accomplish something before contacting me. He said that he knew how much effort I had put forth to ensure his success, and that he wanted to earn a certificate of music from the local community college so that I would be proud of him.

Moment of transparency: I've always lived by the mantra that educators aren't in this field for the *income*, they're in it for the *outcome*. We are fulfilled when we help students achieve a breakthrough moment, whether in mathematics by solving equations, or in chemistry by figuring out which chemicals to use for an experiment.

I can attest that the fulfillment I experienced during that phone call wasn't something I was prepared for or had learned how to handle from a college textbook.

I reassured Jaylen that while I appreciated him striving to achieve his goals and wanting me to see the fruits of my labor, I truly cared for him as a person, and my desire was to ensure that he was safe. Much like parenting, there is nothing that any of my students, past or present, could do to make me mad. I might become disappointed in their actions, but at the end of the day, I will always fight for them and will always seek them out to make sure they have what they need to survive.

Jaylen and I have stayed in contact. I send him a weekly check-in text or FaceTime call. Despite the challenges and setbacks, I can look back and confidently state that the effort I put forth to help him achieve success when he was in high school was worth it. That effort was a seed. I'm now able to sit back and watch Jaylen grow into his purpose on earth as a musician.

WHEN IS ENOUGH, ENOUGH?

Can an educator care too much? I often ask myself this question. There are months when I sit down to pay bills that I discover my checking account balance is lower than I anticipated it would be. As I go line-by-line, I begin to add up the student lunches that I paid, the school fundraisers that I supported, and the list of incidental expenses that I disbursed from my own pocket.

There have been days that I worked ten hours straight at the school, only to drive to the away basketball game because one of my students asked if I was coming. There recently was a week where one student lost his mother due to a terminal illness and another student lost his father due to a suicide. Sometimes it seems like everything occurs back to back, and we can slowly become defeated and deflated.

Let me encourage you: not only should you act as resistance to your students, but you should also make sure you are functioning as a fuse for your own personal life. We have to be cognizant enough to understand when *enough is simply enough*. If you find yourself making rash decisions because you're always tired, or if you find yourself becoming increasingly irritable in the classroom or short-tempered with students, those are key indicators that you need to slow down and prioritize. This is a clear indicator that you need to rest.

You can still donate toward every school fundraiser and attend every basketball game, but make sure you are pacing yourself. Don't go into debt for the sake of a new playground. Instead, figure out ways you can promote the cause to stakeholders and business leaders in the community in order to secure donations. Instead of spending the entire evening at a basketball game, just stay for one half. Or take your papers to grade with you and make an evening of it—and kill two birds with one stone.

At some point in your career, you will encounter tragic situations. When a student is going through challenging situations at home, especially with a sick parent or family member, make sure you avail yourself to them. I believe in treating the student fairly and creating a sense of normalcy for the student, but asking them how they are doing while standing in the lunch line or as they come into the building in the morning can make all the difference.

Instead of always asking how the student is feeling—because we already know the student is sad—ask them if there is anything we can do for them. Inquiring to see if we can take some pressure off the student will establish a level of trust that is almost certain to bud into a positive relationship. Holding students accountable is expected, but showing grace is appreciated.

We all have stories of students like Jaylen. Some might not be as extreme, but situations like these tap into why we chose education in the first place. We certainly didn't do it for the accolades or the recognition. We did it because we see so much more in our students than they often see in themselves.

Someone once said that a graveyard and a prison are the wealthiest places on earth. Each of these places have unwritten best-selling books, undiscovered movie stars, potential professional athletes, and future teachers, doctors, politicians, scientists—and the list goes on...

We must strive each and every day to accomplish our goals and plans, and to help our students achieve theirs. Not fulfilling our purpose or working toward it is not an option. Regret isn't worth it. Our students deserve our best efforts to keep the circuit flowing and to encourage them to reach their highest potential.

FOLLOW-UP QUESTIONS:
CHAPTER SEVEN

1. Are there things in your personal or professional life that you know need some resistance? Do you need to slow down and prioritize your day, week, month, quarter, year?

2. When is it appropriate to stop putting forth effort when helping a student? When is enough, enough?

3. How can you set priorities in your life so that you can give of yourself both personally and professionally to your family and your students?

Chapter Eight

Remembering the Past: Learning the Hard Way

A friend of mine was given an extremely challenging and daunting task. She was hired as the associate director of a non-profit organization and promoted to executive director a few years later.

The former executive director, who was also the founder, was moving to semi-retired status, while serving as the community engagement coordinator. He was responsible for engaging the community in the work of the organization and for soliciting corporate sponsorships for events.

A few months into her new position, my friend was given a directive from the organization's board of directors to terminate this gentleman—the founder of the organization. While she, too, agreed that it was the best decision for the organization so it could move forward under new leadership and fresh vision, it was a significantly uncomfortable assignment.

She once told me that she only gives herself two days to sulk over a negative experience or encounter. She realizes that it's normal and natural to have emotions and to express them when situations arise that might not be comfortable.

After two days, she assesses the interaction and tries to figure out what she can do to learn from the experience. Don't get me wrong, there will be situations that have longer and lingering effects, but it's important to keep the proverbial oars in the water and to keep the boat moving in the right direction.

Have you ever wondered why the rearview mirror in your car is smaller than the front windshield? My thought is fairly simple—where we are headed is more important than where we've been, and we need to see where we're headed.

This isn't to say that we should forget our past experiences. It's simply to say that we should look forward to what's next in our lives: the next school year, the next opportunity, the next vacation, the next work-out, the next meal. Imagine if all we ever focused on was the past—our last year, our last vacation, our last meal, and so forth. While reminiscing over memories very well might bring us joy, it's essential to create new memories and new learning opportunities that will move us forward in life.

While it is important to learn from past mistakes, previous lessons taught, interactions with former students, and conflicts with colleagues and even parents, it is equally, if not more important, to keep moving on.

STICK TO THE RECIPE: BAKE THE CAKE

We will surely encounter situations with our students that frustrate or upset us. It comes with the territory of working with people, especially students. Let's not forget that their brains aren't fully developed yet! We can, and should, have a united mission with our colleagues to help our students, but we must also remember that not every student comes to school to get a quality education. Some students come to school simply because the state mandates it.

It's almost as though we have to put all the ingredients that we're given in August into a mixing bowl and, regardless of the student's learning style or demographic, produce a three-tiered wedding cake by June. Sometimes, the hand we're dealt just simply isn't fair, but we can't limit ourselves or the potential of our students.

One year during my teaching experience, I had 24 freshmen in one social studies class, six of whom had some form of special education plan. While I did have the help of the school intervention specialist, she was already scheduled to be with other students in another part of the building at the same time my class met. I was frustrated beyond belief during the first week of school, because I just couldn't figure out who had scheduled all these students into one class and why they hadn't planned for me to have additional help.

As I considered my options, I realized that I already had the skills needed to modify their lessons and tests. It wasn't necessarily difficult to make these adjustments, but it did require extra time. In the end, I decided that spending those few extra minutes every time I wrote lesson plans was worth it to meet the needs of these students.

As the year progressed, I saw more and more students on special education plans want to be challenged to be able to do the same work that was assigned to the other students.

One parent informed me that her son wanted to take an upcoming test with the other students in the classroom, but he was afraid he would not be able to finish on time. I decided to send the first page of the test home in a sealed envelope with the student the night before the test. His mother would proctor it as a take-home test.

The next day, as I was distributing the test to the class, I gave him just the second page. He finished in about the same amount of time as the other students did with their two-page test. This slowly began to build his confidence, not just as a student, but as a peer.

BULL IN A CHINA SHOP

This might be a hard pill to swallow, but it's okay for educators to apologize. I've made my fair share of mistakes. I once was extremely upset with a classroom full of high school sophomores because of the way they were treating a substitute teacher.

When I received a text from the substitute telling me about their behavior, I rushed down to the classroom and entered the room like a bull in a china shop (shattering everything in its path, and not stopping to think about the consequences).

I was ranting and raving about their behavior and why their actions were very disrespectful. I left the students stunned and fearful after I stepped off my proverbial soapbox and slammed the door on my way out. As the principal, I was dealing with several other issues simultaneously that didn't have anything to do with student discipline, and I really didn't appreciate being interrupted with such nonsense.

Later that night, I reflected on their behavior, and my own. I realized that it was not only unprofessional of me as a principal, but that it put the students in a place of confusion, which was not healthy. My actions had shown the substitute teacher that this type of behavior was acceptable. I knew I would have disciplined a teacher for acting the way I did. I knew I had to correct the situation; it would need more than just a Band-aid on it to cover up my actions—I would have to bring correction to the situation.

The next day, I entered the same classroom calmly and addressed the class. I told them that my words and actions had not been appropriate, and then I humbled myself and apologized. That moment allowed those students to see that while I was in a position of authority and leadership, I could still make mistakes, but I could also take the opportunity to correct those mistakes.

I've apologized to educators and even to parents. I'm not referring to apologizing on behalf of the school, based on how a teacher treated their child; I'm referring to decisions that I made that weren't justified or in the best interest of their child.

Looking back at the episode with the substitute, I recognized that I had been in a very exhausted state. I had been busy preparing for state testing, interviewing teaching candidates for the upcoming school year, and keeping all our state reporting current. All this had caused my own health and fitness to deteriorate. The stress caused by these issues was not an *excuse* for my behavior, but rather an *indicator* that I missed. I had let everything build up to the point that when I was pulled from my office to deal with student discipline, everything came unglued.

The biggest disappointment outside of my own behavior was that it was evident the students hadn't been taught how to act when a substitute teacher was present. This was a situation where we were able to bring about change and move forward, but we had learned the hard way.

DITCH THE WORKSHEETS

While some students loathe having a substitute teacher because it typically means worksheets and silent, sustained reading, other students find great joy in it because it means they can go all out and push every button possible to frustrate the substitute.

We must remember that just like any policy or procedure, if we know we're going to be out of the classroom, it's imperative to outline expectations for our students. Strict enforcement and adherence to these policies will help to ensure effective order and management when we are absent.

We often forget to address the issue of expected student behavior when a substitute teacher will be in the classroom. But just as we teach students other basic classroom behaviors—how to line up at the door, how to respond when called upon, how to retrieve their Chromebook from the cart, and so on—we should teach them how to respond to a substitute teacher.

STUDENTS DESERVE DUE PROCESS

Once, I received an incident report concerning two students who had been engaged in a physical altercation. Because one of the students was a "frequent flyer" and was often in my office for discipline issues, I immediately assumed guilt.

When the students entered my office, I went over what had happened. I assigned one student a consequence, and I suspended the "frequent flyer." I received a phone call later that day from the student's mother. She was expressing concern about why her son had been suspended when he had not instigated the altercation.

After reviewing the situation the next day, I realized that she was correct. I called her and her son in and explained that I had jumped to conclusions, and that I was going to reverse the discipline and remove it from her child's record. The mother was extremely appreciative. The support and attention I showed her helped to develop a level of trust between us, which led to a great working relationship. We were all able to learn from this interaction, and it helped us move forward in dealing with her son's behavior.

LEARNING WITH YOUR STUDENTS

During my first year of teaching, a student asked me a question that pertained to the lesson, and I honestly didn't know the answer. I said, "Let's hold off on questions right now; and if we have time at the end, we'll get to them."

You guessed it: I dragged that lesson out until the bell! I researched the question and was able to answer it the next time the class met. I realized that while I was a subject area guru when it came to social studies, I wasn't an expert. I needed to learn that not knowing the answer was okay.

I decided that the next time a student asked me a question I couldn't answer, I would use it as a learning opportunity for both of us. We would use Chromebooks, cell phones, or even the textbook, and we would research together in order to find the answer we needed. This approach allowed for great discovery in learning, by putting the student in the driver's seat.

While there are situations where we will have to learn the "hard way," the blow can often be softened by allowing our vulnerabilities to be seen. Acknowledging that we acted out of character or admitting that we just don't know something might be perceived as weakness by some, but will be seen by others as simply being human.

It's hard to keep up an image of *perfection*. I would much rather keep up an image of *progression*. A newborn baby goes through the infant stages, then the terrible twos; then before we know it, they are a teenager, on their way to adulthood. *Educators often begin their teaching careers with a textbook understanding of education, but it's the experiential understanding that really produces professional growth.* What matters is not getting stuck where we are, but allowing ourselves to learn and grow along the way.

We have to get to a point where reflection is a part of our routine. There is great benefit in spending a few minutes each day processing the interactions we had with students and parents. It is valuable to assess whether or not our lessons were successful, and how what we're doing today ties into what we did yesterday and what we plan to do tomorrow.

Every time I eat something unhealthy, I find myself saying, "I'm going to start my diet on Monday." I would be in great physical shape if I had actually started dieting on all those Mondays! I challenge you to take advantage of your next "Monday," and make it count! If changes need to be made, the more intentional we are about making them, the more success and improvement we will see not only in our lives, but in the lives of our students, too.

FOLLOW-UP QUESTIONS:
CHAPTER EIGHT

1. What are some ways you process the steps you need to take when you must make a difficult decision pertaining to a student?

2. When you have to "bake the cake"—regardless of the ingredients you are given—and you find yourself underprepared and without the appropriate resources and supports, how can you develop a plan to ensure your students still get to the point of success?

3. Have you ever found yourself in the position of being wrong when interacting with a student, colleague, or parent? Did you apologize? What steps did you take to correct the situation?

Chapter Nine

The Dash Effect

Someone once asked me, "What's the most important part of a tombstone?" I considered answering that it was the birth date, but then I realized that everyone had one, so the only uniqueness would be the time in world history in which the deceased had been born. I considered answering that it was the death date, but again, everyone had one. The name was probably important, and so was the scripture verse or the quote that might be engraved on the stone.

After I finished running through the gauntlet of options, the person told me that the dates weren't nearly as important as everything that had happened *between* those dates. In essence, the "dash" between the dates was the most important part.

This illustration is simple, yet profound. We are all given the same 24 hours in a day, the same 1,440 minutes in a day, and the same 86,400 seconds in a day. It's not the time that makes the difference; it's what we do with that time that makes the difference. When we are fulfilling our life's purpose on earth, we have the opportunity to make the greatest impact with the time we have been given.

PERFECTION IS POSSIBLE

We have all had that one teacher in school who made all the difference for us. It might have been because they acknowledged us, or because their excitement about teaching made us want to come to school and learn. Or, perhaps we sensed that they were invested in us as students.

For me, that teacher was Mr. Trocchia. Mr. Trocchia was an older Italian man who taught my high school choir class. He had been with the school district since its inception in the 1960s, and he was solely responsible for writing the school's fight song and alma mater. Under his leadership, the marching band and the choral programs became recognized at both state and national levels for earning high marks in competitions.

He was a very determined educator. He didn't *expect*, he *demanded* our absolute best in our participation in the school's vocal and instrumental music programs. There were three vocal ensembles at my high school, with a combined total of nearly 150 students. During my sophomore year, I auditioned for the top choir that only had 32 spots.

I will never forget rushing over to the auditorium door during lunch to see if my name was on the posted list of students who had earned a spot that year. When I saw my name on the roster, I found a quarter in my bookbag and rushed to call my mom on the payphone in the cafeteria to tell her. I had wanted so badly to sit under Mr. Trocchia's direction and leadership. Through hard work and commitment, I was finally afforded the opportunity.

Mr. Trocchia's performance groups earned unanimous superior ratings for forty consecutive years at all competitions, which meant that every vocal or instrumental group that he took to a competition scored in the highest of five categories based on the rating system. Mr. Trocchia kept telling us during my sophomore year that perfect was possible. He would prepare and overprepare for each 40-minute daily rehearsal. He had our rehearsals planned to the minute.

We would listen to music from professional choir ensembles, and then he would expect that not only would we be able sing it, regardless of the challenge, but we would be able to sing it better than the recording.

That year, we were preparing for the final competition of his teaching career, and he had white T-shirts made for us. Our group name was on the front of the shirt; on the back of the shirt was a treble clef with the phrase, "Perfection is Possible."

We drove to West Virginia to sing for a panel of judges, professional musicians and music educators who were going to score and rate our performance. The pressure was immense, as this was the final group that Mr. Trocchia was taking to compete. We didn't want to be known as the group that broke the unanimous superior rating streak that had lasted for 40 years!

We sang our hearts out that day. When we received our score sheet back, we learned that we had not only received a unanimous superior rating from every single judge, but we had also received a "superior plus" rating from one of the judges. This wasn't even a possible category or rating, but the judges deemed our performance worthy of a perfect score.

Outside of the building, Mr. Trocchia said, as he welled up with pride, "I told you that perfection was possible." That was one of the greatest moments of my high school experience. Mr. Trocchia was solely responsible for creating that moment, but it wasn't just a moment that lasted for an hour; it was a moment that lives on today. I knew then that I wanted to be an educator so that I could create experiences for my students just like Mr. Trocchia did for me.

You can, too! Ask yourself: What am I doing every day to create these types of experiences and memories for my students? Am I digging deep into the recesses of my creativity and designing lesson plans that inspire students? Am I challenging and demanding the best out of my students?

As you think back to the experiences you had with the teachers in your school: what set *that* teacher apart for me and what am I doing to become *that* teacher for my students today?

LIVE OUT YOUR DASH

I have been determined to live my life—my "dash"— to the fullest extent by having as big an impact as I can on my students. While I was driving home one weekend during my freshman year of college, I remember telling myself that all I wanted in life was to be influential and effective. At that time, I was majoring in political science, so my thought was that I would become a politician and help to create a positive change locally or state-wide.

I look back and laugh now because the purpose for my life is to serve in education, but I've also been provided with the opportunity to be both influential and effective. I've discovered that most of the time, it's been in the one-on-one settings. In my opinion, this has yielded greater fulfillment to my life than having a microphone in a campaign rally and begging for votes would have had.

While there are times we all secretly envy the teachers that go viral for dancing on their students' desks or for being featured on a talk show, what we can't fail to realize is that making an impact simply means making a connection. Some of our impact moments might be in group settings, but the majority of the influence we will have is in our one-on-one dealings with our students. It's these interactions that will not only shape the trajectory of their lives but will allow us to have a fulfilled sense of purpose. It will make all those dreaded college student loan payments finally worth it!

One way you can tell the age of a tree is by cutting it down and counting the number of rings on the stump. A sapling and a tree that is 100 years old are similar in nature, but they have two different levels of impact. A sapling is a young tree, small enough to be planted in a cup and left on a window ledge. It often has to be held up with a wooden stake until it's able to grow on its own.

As the tree goes through the maturation process, it knows how to seek the light, and it knows how to fulfill its function—whether it's an apple tree, a maple tree, or the like. When trees are tall enough, they are able to provide shade for those hot summer days. When they are mature enough, they will produce apples we can eat or fragrant blossoms that we can enjoy. Over time, a tree grows into the purpose for which it was planted.

We will often not realize the impact that we make on our students until years later. As educators, we want to create those memorable experiences for our students, and we want to figure out if the relationships we've created are having an impact. Just like the trees, though, it often takes time before the student will have a full understanding of the level of care and commitment that we provided for them.

Many times, it is not until a student moves to a new school or goes on to college that they see how much we cared, how much we invested in them, and how much we fought for their future success.

It's in those moments, the moments when former students who are home on break stop by the school to see how we're doing that we're able to sit back and reap the dividend of the investment we made years before. These students always seem to show up on the days we need the encouragement the most. Just think—of every possible place they could be on their break, they chose to come right back to our classroom. Those can truly be humbling moments.

In tough times, remember, that just like a tree, we come into the fruition of our purpose as an educator over time. When a farmer plants a crop, there is a period of waiting before he can harvest it. The seeds that were planted aren't waiting, they're in the process of working. We just can't see them doing their jobs. We have to be determined enough, but also patient enough, to trust the process.

DIFFERENTIATED RELATIONSHIPS

We have many different relationships in our lives—family members, friends, spouse, children. Each relationship is different, and each one requires a different commitment.

We only open ourselves up to a certain degree with our acquaintances at work, but we are usually comfortable enough to "let our hair down" when it comes to our best friends or relatives. These are the individuals who know more about us than people like our work associates who only know us on a more surface level. In order to live our "dash," we must live authentic lives, while understanding the parameters of each of our relationships.

In a similar fashion, we must take into consideration the various types of students we have in our classroom: their different learning styles, social abilities, and demographics. While a classroom should have a standard set of rules and procedures, with corresponding consequences, our interaction with every student should be differentiated based on what it is they need in order to be successful.

By no means do I think teachers should "walk on eggshells" when dealing with challenging students. Rather, we should interact with and create plans for students based on their performance in the classroom. For instance, if we know that a student is introverted and shy, we should not call on that student to read aloud in front of the entire class. Instead, we can figure out a way to include that student in the classroom environment, perhaps by having them be the line leader or the attendance taker.

At the same time, if we have a very rambunctious student who always seems to be talking, we can create ways for that student to burn off some energy. For instance, we can have that student run an errand to the farthest point in the building, or ask them to walk around and return graded papers. We could even have them stand at the front of the room to read aloud.

We also must be careful and considerate of the emotional needs of students. Referring back to holistic education, we need to know our students. Understanding the parent dynamic is a key starting point for establishing a strong relationship. Knowing if the student eats breakfast and lunch, checking to see what is preventing the student from completing homework, and seeking to understand why the student is always so tired are ways that will help us as an educator in the long-run, while helping the student in the process.

I enjoy taking site visits to successful schools across the country. I'm often intrigued by the technology integration, the classroom designs, and the presentation of the school. By presentation, I'm referring to the branding and the overall feeling and sense of pride I get when I walk through the door. If I walk into a school and can sense that there is a strong culture of pride, then I know that the teachers and students will be excited to come to work and school each day.

There's no greater sense of pride than attending an event like a pep rally where everyone has the same goal—to cheer their team on to victory! When all the people groups of a school are fully engaged, and they are bringing the mission of the school to life, the school is effectively living out its "dash." This is also a true testament to a great school administration.

As an educator, it's important that we take account of our brand and our identity. I'm not referring to our personal websites and logos; I'm referring to how our students identify us. For example, there is a teacher in my building who has a long-standing reputation for being strict. He doesn't tolerate or deal with any nonsense during his instruction. That's the brand that he's created.

I've also encountered a teacher whom the students labeled the "cool teacher." Later, I came to learn that this meant that fun was more important than learning, which proved to become somewhat detrimental.

Each of us has our own identity. We will be known for our personality quirks, whether or not our lessons are exciting, and, most importantly, how we treat our students and how they feel in our presence. We have to create this identity all while making sure we are living out our "dash."

I'm reminded of a school administrator who shared once that how people answer the phone makes an enormous difference. At first, I assumed he meant that our school administrative assistants should be equipped with the proper phone extensions and calendars to better answer the questions that parents might have. What he meant was, "Answer your phone with a smile, because smiles are contagious, and people can sense your happiness."

Of course, like many, I thought this was a crazy way to think, until I had to pay my cable bill and was stuck with an account representative who seemed undeniably miserable. She wasn't pleasant, she barely greeted me before reading her obligatory script, and I almost had to close the call out on my own after I paid my bill. She seemed decidedly unhappy, and I could sense it.

On the other hand, people can also feel when someone is being friendly, not out of obligation, but out of genuine care and concern. We remember how waitresses treat us; we remember how flight attendants treat us; we remember how store employees treat us.

We need to keep in mind that our students, parents, and colleagues remember how we treat them. If we seem hurried or uninterested in something a parent is bringing to our attention, it shows. If we are rushing a student to answer a question because we're tired of standing, it shows. If we respond out of annoyance to a fellow teacher in a staff meeting when they've suggested something that the school should implement, it shows. Simply put, people remember how they're treated, and they remember how we make them feel.

While experiences might shape how we perceive something, it's going to be the relationships that we forged with our students that will ultimately determine how others will remember our "dash." Being understanding and showing empathy to students might mean the world to them. Listening to a student as they explain an answer the long way, yet in a way they understand, helps to build their confidence. Cheering on a student at a football or basketball game when you know their parents had to work that evening can make a student feel valued and special.

We must aspire to become the difference for our students. *Becoming the difference* happens when we seek to *understand the different*. Then, we are truly living out our "dash."

FOLLOW-UP QUESTIONS:
CHAPTER NINE

1. Who was the most influential teacher in your life? What qualities and characteristics classified this teacher as the most influential?

2. Are you fulfilling your life's purpose on earth by living out your "dash?" What are you doing daily, weekly, and monthly to make sure you stay on task and track to live out your "dash"?

3. Outside of academics, what are some practical ways that you can differentiate your relationships with students, while still remaining professional and fair to everyone?

Chapter Ten

It's Not What We Say,
It's What We Do

"**N**ever let them see you smile—at least not until Christmas!" This was the advice I received from a veteran teacher when I was first starting out in education. This teacher was speaking from her nearly 25 years of classroom experience. At first, I was able to understand her logic. I knew the value of establishing a strong classroom management plan and making sure students learned my expectations and procedures.

However, I slowly began to realize how backward that philosophy sounded. I kept hearing other educators discussing the importance of developing positive relationships with students at the onset of the school year. I've very rarely sought to develop a relationship with someone that doesn't involve a smile or a laugh.

It might take a while for my class to finally grasp hold of my policies, but holding my students hostage to an unenthusiastic (and unpleasant) teacher for four months of the school year was simply unfair for both my students and me. We *can* teach expectations and establish a high standard of discipline—and do so while bringing a level of excitement through ingenuity and innovation.

I believe we must model the behaviors and attitudes we want our students to emulate. If we show up to work every day putting on a front that we are tough and that school isn't fun, we can't get upset with our students when they respond to our instruction in the same manner.

IDEAS AND INTENTIONS

Have you ever been out shopping and overheard a parent reprimanding their child? And have you ever pretended you were shopping for something in that section of the store just so you could see and hear what's going on?

Time and time again, I have heard a parent tell their child to stop doing something, or there will be a consequence. What I always get confused about is why the parent has to say it over and over. If they were really going to give the child a consequence, why didn't they go ahead and implement it after the first or second warning?

I call these types of interactions "hollow threats." While words can show our ideas, actions show our intentions. Without the actions, there is no substance to the threat. There is nothing to back up our original statement. Unfortunately for teachers, students have become proficient at recognizing these types of threats. It can often create a situation that leads to us having a very long school year, especially with students who exhibit behavior issues.

I often train new teachers to understand the value of their first interaction with their students. The first few days of a school year will make or break the rest of the school year. If a teacher loses control of the class on the first day of school, they'll spend the next 179 school days trying to get it back.

When a student violates a stated policy, we need to assign a consequence. Having a conversation is absolutely necessary and will typically help curtail future issues, but it's imperative that we maintain control of the classroom. This isn't done effectively by yelling and screaming at students, but by following our plan.

Students have been through enough teachers in their school experience that they can usually get a strong reading on whether or not they will like us as a teacher. This assessment doesn't take them long to make.

Students learn from teachers they like. Students also will perform their best for teachers they believe care about their well-being. I'm in no way insinuating that teachers should put on a front in order to gain likability points from their students, but I'm saying that our words and actions during the trust-building stage of our classroom relationships need to be very strategic.

When we gather twenty random students into a classroom and we're supposed to make magic happen in the next 180 days, we will inevitably encounter student personalities that will intentionally defy us or, to be frank, just get on our nerves. The true character and personalities of our students will begin to show in the classroom within the first few days of school. Allow students to be true to who they are, but only allow them to do so within the confines of classroom expectations. Treat every student the same, by treating them fairly and in accordance with the classroom management and discipline systems.

PAY UP: $100 LATER

I'm reminded of something that happened with one of my students named Avonti. We were on the annual senior trip to Orlando and stumbled upon an interactive aquapark that included a wakeboarding course. Our school is located in the city, so most of our students have only had basic waterpark experiences, with standard attractions such as slides and a swimming pool.

Wakeboarding was new, interesting, and challenging. Wakeboarding is similar to waterskiing, but instead of being towed by a boat, you are pulled forward by a series of overhead cables while you are kneeling or standing on a board which resembles a surfboard. Our students enjoyed it so much that we went back for more—during the six hours we had between checking out of our hotel and getting to the airport on time!

Our entire group was struggling trying to grasp the techniques of wakeboarding. The operator would hand the guided cable rope to the next person on the dock.

When the light turned green, that person knew it was their turn. The cable was going to pull them off the dock and out into the water. It was up to them to position their body, maintain their balance and form, and stay on the board. The farthest anyone in our group made it before ending up in the water was an average of about fifteen feet.

I decided to spice things up a little. I told the group that if anyone made it around the lake just one time, I would give them $100. You would be surprised at the level of determination the students exhibited from that moment forward! Students were making it farther than they ever had, beyond the fifteen-foot mark and around the first turn before they crashed and burned. I still couldn't make it past fifteen feet.

Then we noticed that Avonti had effortlessly rounded the first turn. We cheered him on as he slowly rounded the second turn. Little did he know that the 90 degree turn that even experienced riders struggled with was just ahead. We collectively held our breath as he navigated the swift 90 degree turn and made his way back to the dock. The seniors were elated for him. The first person he sought after he got out of the water and back onto the dock was me. You guessed it—he wanted his $100! I didn't have the cash on me, but I promised him that I would get the money to him once we got back to Ohio.

We flew home later that day. Once we touched down, deplaned, and headed to the baggage claim area, he looked at me and said, "You do know what state we're in now, right?" I smiled and told him that I would have his $100 on Monday. Secretly, I was hoping he would forget.

The seniors only had about five days of school left at that point, and I just knew that he would be so focused on his final exams that he wouldn't mention it to me again. I was wrong—so wrong! He kept mentioning it, and I just kept forgetting to stop by the ATM after work. On the last day of school, I told Avonti that I would just have to mail it to him.

Graduation day arrived, and after the graduates had entered the auditorium, as the principal, I was the first person to speak. I welcomed the graduates and their guests, and I shared four or five highlights that pertained to the graduating class.

I shared that once again we had a 100% graduation rate, a 100% college placement rate, and that our graduates had been offered more money in college scholarships than any other graduating class in school history. I shared about our boys' basketball team winning the state championship, and about how some of our visual art students were featured in a national publication.

Then the big moment arrived. I had decided a few moments before heading to the school that evening that I would acknowledge Avonti in a humorous way for being our first-ever "Watersport Champion" by successfully making his way around the wakeboarding course. I told the audience that I had put $100 on the line, and that we had one graduate who had defied the odds and made his way around the course with ease.

I also stated that because I'm a man of my word, I wanted to present Avonti with a crisp, new $100 bill. I asked him to come forward, and the crowd stood and cheered, applauding his accomplishment. I knew, though, that this was a learning moment. The graduates would understand that while what I said was important, it was even more important that I followed through with the requisite actions.

MEAN WHAT YOU SAY

The easiest way to lose the respect of our students is to say one thing and do something else. If we say we're going to do something, we should do it. This doesn't pertain just to student discipline, but to other situations as well: attending after school sporting events, tutoring a student during lunch, supporting their fundraisers.

It is certainly acceptable to allow for grace when situations occur that are beyond the control of the student. There is wisdom in communicating with the student about the situation, but we must be consistent with our policies. For instance, if our homework policy states that there is a 10-point penalty for work turned in late, still deduct the points. If we have a policy that indicates a parent phone call after a student has to be redirected three times, then follow through with a phone call. Remember that being fair, positive, and consistent go a long way.

For some of our students, the only stability they might experience is with us when they come to school. It's essential that we develop a routine for our students from the time they enter our classroom until it's time for them to leave. Because some students will be faced with uncertainty in their home lives, it's imperative that we provide that needed stability and structure. Within that structure comes a level of discipline that is needed for academic success.

Every school or district has their own policy when it comes to student discipline. While students equate discipline with bad behavior, we must be consistent with them because we know that discipline is really the practice of training our students to follow the rules and procedures. It's when they fail to adhere to the rules and procedures that they face a consequence that might not be favorable in their eyes.

Parents don't discipline their children with the intent to harm them. They do so to make them better or stronger. We must work to ensure that our students understand this concept and how it applies in the classroom. Little children might hate brushing their teeth, even though there is great benefit in doing so at a young age, but they won't understand the value of it until much later in life.

Any discipline we assign should have a purpose. I've never understood the strategy in implementing consequences such as an after-school detention. It might help prevent a certain behavior from occurring, but it doesn't fix the root of the behavior issue. I've noticed that the only students this truly affects are students who have athletic practices or part-time jobs after school. Do I want a student to receive a write-up at their job because I forced them to stay after school for a detention? Surely, there is a better approach.

If a student keeps forgetting their pencil, instead of continuing to assign them a lunch detention or taking away their recess, figure out a way to help them remember to bring their pencil to class. Better yet, keep a pencil tucked away somewhere just for them.

Taking away opportunities like recess, gym, music and so forth are not the solution. For some students, these experiences might be exactly what they need in order to make it through the day. If a student needs to burn off energy, why would we keep them inside during recess? We are told that differentiating our instruction will better meet the needs of our students, but why is it that we don't differentiate our discipline to meet the needs of our students?

Students will respond when they see that our actions come from a place of care and consideration. They are watching and listening even when we don't realize it. We must strive to model the behavior we want to see in our students—and it begins in the classroom.

CONTENT AND DELIVERY

The attitude and manner in which we relay information is just as important as the content that is being delivered. Being truthful is essential, but understanding a situation and knowing whether we should show empathy or compassion should be considered. For example, if a student is acting out because they are dealing with the loss of a parent, we should seek to understand what the immediate needs of the student are that we can help resolve.

However, if a student is intentionally bullying or showing hatred toward another student, yes, we should seek to get to the root of the issue, but our conversation and tone are probably going to be much sterner, and our words should mirror those of our student handbook.

Once the student has fulfilled their consequence, the class has resumed as normal, and the discipline issue has been resolved, do not address or bring up the issue to the student again. If our interaction with the student was effective during the discipline process, then we will have found ways to help the student learn and grow from their misjudgment or mistake.

It is important to speak to the student privately and not in the presence of their peers when they return to class. We can let them know that we care for them and that we are going to make sure they stay on track with their behavior. We should also make sure that the student knows that being assigned a discipline consequence doesn't mean we like them any less.

Regardless of what our students might have said or done, they deserve to come to school and be engaged in a culture in the classroom that shows them that we care for them and have their best interest at heart. We can't be too quick to assume the worst. Students have bad days, just like we do. We can allow these interactions with them to serve as learning opportunities. And remember, in all our communication with students, to make sure we treat them fairly and with dignity.

FOLLOW-UP QUESTIONS:
CHAPTER TEN

1. What is your procedure for establishing a well-managed classroom at the onset of the school year?

2. What do you think are the reasons why a teacher makes "hollow threats" when dealing with discipline issues?

3. How do you retract something you've said to a student that was more harmful than helpful, while still maintaining their trust?

Chapter Eleven

You Don't Have to Be Seen to Be Heard

Nothing brightens my day more than when I drive up to the window at Starbucks, and the cashier says, "The person in front of you paid for your coffee today!" It gives me a little glimmer of hope that there are still good people left in this crazy world.

SMALL CONNECTIONS; BIG IMPACT

I was recently in Florida for a week of rest and relaxation. As I was driving to get one of my favorite key lime pie milkshakes, I had to stop for a red light. I noticed two people, whom I presumed to be homeless, standing on the corner. One person was holding a sign asking for money, and the other person was smiling and waving at the cars. I had seen people holding cardboard signs before, but I had never seen a homeless person waving and smiling like that. So, I grabbed about a dollar's worth of loose change that I had left over from the toll roads and handed it to the woman before the light changed.

A few minutes later, I pulled into the restaurant drive-through to order my milkshake. As I started to pull around the building to pay, the cashier said, "It's on us today. We just wanted to thank you for being a customer."

"Did the person in front of me pay for my order?" I asked.

"No, we just wanted to thank you for your patronage!"

At that moment, I thought about the money I had given to the lady on the corner. That small favor was being returned to me by the restaurant. That $3.49 milkshake made my entire day!

The power to create these same types of experiences for our students is within our grasp. It starts by becoming connected with our students and by being cognizant of their needs. One way we can become aware of their needs is by being aware of their behavior. I'm not referring to students acting out of line or breaking the rules; I'm referring to their behavior in general. If a student is being insubordinate, that's one thing, but if a student is sleeping during class, that's an entirely different type of behavior that needs to be addressed.

It's the little things we do that make a big difference. If we notice that a student doesn't have lunch money, making them feel comfortable and letting them know they can still go through the lunch line will speak volumes. This helps to establish a level of trust.

Drawing attention to or humiliating a student who doesn't have money for lunch is never acceptable. Asking the student to come to our desk while the entire class is working in groups or meeting with the student privately in the back of the classroom are ways in which we can eliminate the embarrassment factor.

We should be mindful of whether other students nearby could overhear our conversation. We in no way want to embarrass the student, so it falls on us to think creatively when we seek to help a student in need.

I have even gone as far as writing the question on a piece of paper: "Do you have lunch money?" and then having the student come up to my desk to "clarify an answer from a homework assignment."

I asked, "Please clarify if this is a yes or a no." I've discovered that students will be honest, and will feel relieved, when they see that we really want to help them.

The same concept can apply to a student who needs school supplies or hygiene items. Simply seeing the need and finding a way to meet that need without bringing unnecessary attention to our actions will allow us to make a big impact. Although it might seem like a small thing to us, it can seem like a huge thing to a student.

EFFECTIVELY COMMUNICATING WITHOUT WORDS

Growing up, my parents occasionally gave me "the look." This look told me they weren't pleased with my conduct, whether I was acting out at a family gathering or nodding off at a wedding. To me, getting "the look" was just as powerful as being reprimanded by my parents.

123

Much of our communication is nonverbal. Nonverbal communication, put simply, is our body language—what our body is saying to others. We may not think much about what our facial expressions are communicating or what our posture and tone of voice are conveying.

But our students know how we feel by the way we look at them. If we have a look of disdain or irritation, students can feel it. If we are constantly shaking our heads or crossing our arms in frustration, students can feel it. If we are smirking or rolling our eyes when a student has attempted to answer a question four times and still can't provide the correct answer, students can feel it.

It is never acceptable to demean a student because they don't understand a concept, even if we've taught the concept multiple times. One more reteaching moment might just do the trick.

Humiliating a student in front of their peers can set the student back farther than we realize. It might cause them to refrain from answering questions or participating in class discussions in the future because of the humiliation they felt in the past.

Some teachers have moved to using nonverbal signals or cues for classroom transitions. This can help immensely when the classroom environment needs to be quiet and conducive for all learners. Simply holding up a hand or a certain number of fingers might signify to the class that it is time to put their work away and silently line up for lunch. These strategies can be very productive, especially when there is strong order and management within the classroom.

INNOVATIVE TEACHING: BOOK CAFÉ

While teachers are an important part of the classroom environment, they are not always the be-all and end-all of the learning environment. Direct instruction is necessary and needed for certain content and in certain environments. Putting the responsibility of learning into the hands of students—while the teacher acts as a guide—is a concept more and more schools are embracing today.

I came to the school one day and noticed that Mrs. Boggs, the middle school English teacher, was wearing what appeared to be a waitress outfit. I assumed it was a themed day or a spirit day that I had forgotten to put on my calendar.

Later that morning when I was visiting classrooms, I noticed that there was a sign outside her door reading, "Welcome to the Boggs Book Café." I looked into Mrs. Boggs' classroom and saw that it had been transformed into a beautiful café!

Mrs. Boggs was dressed as a waitress and had asked the students to wait while she seated them at the tables. The tables were covered in traditional red and white checkered tablecloths, with flowers placed perfectly in the center. There was a place setting and menu at every seat. On the menu were the assignments that the students had to work on during class. She visited each table, asking if the students needed any help with their menu options.

She had created a level of suspense for her students, and I would almost guarantee that her students couldn't wait to tell their parents about their experience in her classroom that day. Mrs. Boggs didn't use words to teach the concepts of the lesson that day. Instead, she put the students right in the middle of the learning event by creating an experience for them. This type of excitement creates a buzz in our schools and makes a significant impact on student learning.

I secretly loathe worksheets. The only real value in them—in my opinion—is to be able to keep students on track during the lesson. Assigning a worksheet that involves very little innovation or critical thinking is not a beneficial use of student time. I feel the same way about having students answer the questions at the end of a chapter in the textbook. These types of assignments are more appropriate for individual student enrichment, or review for a quiz or test, than they are as a part of general classroom instruction.

Engagement through creative lab experiences or through assignments that integrate technology or group discussions demonstrate to students that we have spent time preparing the lesson for them. When I walk by a classroom and sense chaos—only to realize the noise is as a result of innovative learning—I always stop in and see what they are studying. I never ask the students to quiet down, and I give extra praise to the teachers who created these structured environments for energized learning. They deserve the credit because creating and managing these scenarios is often like hugging a tornado—hard to do and hard to keep on track.

CREATIVE COMMUNICATION

"Have you cleaned your bedroom yet?"

"Have you taken out the trash yet?"

"Is your homework finished?"

We were asked these same questions over and over again when we were kids. Many times, the answer was "no." We just didn't find any fun in it, so we drug our feet getting our chores done, and tuned out our parents when they asked us these questions.

The same is true in education. There comes a point where students tune us out because they know what's coming. They are quick to figure out our routines and procedures.

When we teach in creative ways and present content in nontraditional methods, we often engage students of all learning styles. Students are excited to see what we have up our sleeves next. Students are more apt to remember a learning experience, a field trip, a guest speaker, or a project-based learning assignment versus direct instruction.

Much of what our students are learning in education today is rote memorization of facts, key dates, names, and places. Just because we had to write out the bold terms from our textbooks as kids and define them on a sheet of lined notebook paper doesn't mean that our students should have to do the same thing. Why should we require our students to learn in the same way that was relevant a decade or more ago?

Traditional direct instruction and textbook usage both have their place in education. There is a benefit to all types of instruction. The challenge we are presented with today is to create learning experiences that will live on in the minds of our students. Our students deserve to be motivated to learn, and we are doing them a disservice when we take the easy route.

It's up to us to do the things that have a lasting impact. It's up to us to make sure our words and our body language are saying the same thing. It's up to us to create opportunities for students both to learn and to have fun in the process!

FOLLOW UP QUESTIONS:
CHAPTER ELEVEN

1. What are some small adjustments you can make in your communication style that might yield a greater student response?

2. How can students in your classroom sense your temperament?

3. What are the pros and cons of flipping instruction and putting students in the driver's seat of their education?

Chapter Twelve

Creatures of Habit: Caring More About the Future

I have to admit that I often find myself binging on YouTube videos about the most random and obscure topics. I recently watched a video about a group of millennials who were interns on a television talk show. They were being quizzed by the show's host about various vintage objects and how to use them.

One of the items the host held up to a young lady was a rotary phone. The intern knew it was a phone, but she became perplexed when asked to dial a number, and wasn't able to complete the challenge. I was disappointed, but had to remind myself that just as I have never experienced a telephone "party line," this intern had never experienced using a rotary phone— simply because of when she was born.

TAKING IT ALL FOR GRANTED

We can become so accustomed to a way of life that we can't even imagine what life would be like if things were different. Or, we don't even think about what life would be like without certain things, because we take them for granted.

I remember when I bought my very first cell phone as a sophomore in high school. The phone was a flip-phone model, and the screen was green. I even upgraded my plan in order to be able to use the texting feature. There were no such things as emojis, and phones did not yet come with cameras.

About a year after I purchased my phone, I began hearing people talk about how cell phones would soon be equipped with Internet capability. Fast-forward two decades and look at what cell phones can do today! We can take and send pictures and videos any time we want. We can complete work for our jobs and take classes using our phones. We can even broadcast "live" from our living rooms to the world.

Like phones, vehicles have become better equipped and more technology based.

I remember helping a relative move back to our hometown from her college apartment. It was June, and the temperature was around 90 degrees that day. We had packed a small moving truck with her furniture and belongings and were ready to head out. I sat down in the truck and reached over to turn on the air conditioning—and discovered that there wasn't any! It had never occurred to us when we rented the truck that some of the older models didn't come with air conditioning.

This was what people often jokingly refer to as a "first-world problem"—a luxury we felt we couldn't live without, but most certainly could. As we were pulling out of the apartment complex on campus, my uncle laughed as he yelled to us, "There is air conditioning in that truck! It's called "4-60 AC." Put all four windows down and drive 60 miles per hour!"

When we all got back home, my uncle told us how none of the vehicles had air conditioning when he was growing up. Being from a different generation, though, our experience was quite different.

The amenities that were standard on vehicles have advanced over time. Being confident enough to embrace the innovations on not only our cars and cell phones, but on our other technologies, has helped to create simpler and more effective—and often faster—ways to live life and fulfill our obligations.

As technology continues to evolve, we must remember that students today have been born into a world that looks much different than it did when we were in school. In order for our students to become competitive with those in the world after graduation, it has become imperative that we figure out ways to assimilate these elements into our instruction and daily routines.

CHANGE IS INEVITABLE – 1:1 + 1

Innovation: when I first heard of this concept, my thought was that *innovation* was simply the integration of technology into the classroom.

When a school is labeled as a 1:1 school, it means that the school has a computer or other electronic device for every student. This has become the new normal in education. Alluding to technology as a "bad" thing and placing little to no value on it creates the opportunity for there to be a disconnect between staff and students. We don't have to integrate technology into everything, but we should learn to embrace it.

I remember when I first started teaching, I had both a Smart Board and an overhead projector in my classroom. Because I was accustomed to seeing teachers use an overhead projector when I was in school, I was more drawn to it than to the Smart Board. I had to realize that I was quickly going to become obsolete. I needed to make the shift to the newer technology in order to provide what was best for my students.

Innovation is not simply *using* technology, but rather, it is *how we go about using* technology in order to create a more effective way of doing things. Technology should never replace or become the teacher in our classrooms. It should serve as an enhancement to what is already taking place.

An example that I often share with other educators is that a Chromebook should not become a $499 version of a written assignment. Instead, we should seek to figure out how we can use the Chromebook to innovate the assignment. For instance, instead of providing a printed ten-question multiple choice quiz, we could have students use the Chromebook to create a video demonstrating mastery of the academic content standard. This is true innovation.

I recently attended a leadership conference. One of the presenters described how students see thousands of images during the course of their day. It's likely that students will be watching TV, playing a game on their phones, or looking at social media all in the span of just a few minutes. Flipping through channels, scrolling through social media, and opening and closing apps occurs much more frequently than we realize.

The speaker noted the fact that our students have become so overstimulated with images that they struggle with sitting still and listening to their teacher speak for a forty-minute lecture. He didn't say that we should steer away from traditional direct instruction, but that we must be creative in our delivery to ensure that we keep the attention of our students.

Becoming familiar with the ever-evolving and ever-changing world can be a job all by itself, but doing so will definitely create a connection that will allow us to better understand today's students at their level. It doesn't hurt to stay caught up with the latest trends, even when they do not pertain to technology. Asking them about their current fashion fads and even their latest lingo, which is often humorous, helps us keep up with and have a better understanding of what they're saying, thinking, and doing.

I like to think of the 1:1 model as 1:1 + 1. One device for every student, plus the teacher. When we exclude the teacher from the equation, the technology becomes the key source of curriculum, and even, at times, the teacher.

USING TWITTER AS YOUR TEACHER

What would happen if you tried to put on a pair of jeans from high school? Assuming that you graduated twenty years ago, I'm going to go out on a limb and guess that the pants won't fit as they once did. And I'm sure the style of the pants is now outdated. Yet we hang on to them, hoping they will come back in style!

But as time moves on, we have to make changes that accommodate the advances. As educators, we can't be afraid to move forward and think differently than educators did even just a few years ago. We must see the future and the innovation in education as a positive thing. Most importantly, as our students see us taking risks and modeling this behavior, they will be more likely to do the same.

Even if we fail at first when we are trying something new, we have to understand that there are still learning moments in our failure. No one intentionally sets out for failure when they are presenting content in a new way or when they are modifying a lesson to integrate technology or videos. We know how to capitalize on these moments when our students experience failure; we need to apply the same grace and acceptance to ourselves when we fail.

When I was a freshman in college, I moved back home at the semester change. My tuition bill was paid, and my grades were good, but I just wasn't ready for the college environment. After I moved back in with my mother, I began attending a branch campus of one of the major universities in my city.

I was initially discouraged and felt as though I had failed, but my grandmother reminded me this occurrence wasn't a loss; it was an experience. My time in the dorm and living on campus allowed me to gain the experience needed to share with students today the do's and don'ts of what it takes to live away from home.

There are a plethora of online professional learning communities for educators on social media today, especially on Twitter. Becoming part of a community of fellow educators can help you stay current with new and innovative strategies and ideas for the classroom.

I was engaged in a chat recently on Twitter with a group of educators. I soon realized that I had no idea what they were tweeting about, so I googled the instructional model they were discussing. I could have simply logged out and gone on with my evening; but instead, I decided to continue the research on my own and have my own free professional development workshop from the comfort of my living room couch!

I've also discovered that most educators will jump at the opportunity to share a new idea or best practice with colleagues. We will often ignore areas that we know aren't our strengths, but that won't help us progress and move forward. Staying truthful to my need to learn new things, such as my example with the Twitter chat, has helped me continue to grow as a leader in education, which then helps my teachers become better equipped for their students.

MOMENTS OF HONESTY & GROWTH

When I assumed the high school principal role at my school nearly a decade ago, I was sharing with a mentor who had been in education for nearly 30 years that I was struggling to build a connection with some of the teachers. There were teachers on staff whose careers were twice or even three times as long as mine. It made for some intimidating conversations.

I shared with him that I found it so challenging to connect with some of the veteran teachers that when it came time for their annual evaluations, I stressed myself out and was hesitant to present anything to these teachers that might prompt a difficult discussion. I often found myself simply highlighting their strengths and encouraging them to continue working hard for the betterment of our students.

My mentor encouraged me to think of ways that I could personally and professionally add value to the more veteran teachers. He told me to write a list of my strengths and slowly begin to integrate those topics into conversations and evaluations.

One thing that occurred to me was that while I knew that some of these teachers dreaded technology, I didn't. I discovered that one reason they didn't use it in the classroom was because they just didn't know how. Added to that, they were afraid of what the students would say if they didn't appear proficient.

I began to make concerted efforts to encourage teachers to integrate technology into their lessons and modeled the behavior for them to see. One of the teachers agreed to add a Chromebook cart to his classroom. His students can now conduct research right in the classroom instead of going to the computer lab.

Small steps matter, and small steps make a difference—small steps are still steps! When we first jump into a swimming pool, we are usually shocked by the temperature of the water. As our body acclimates to the water, we eventually stop shivering from the cold and can venture away from the side of the pool and enjoy the swimming experience.

The same is true when making adjustments in our instructional methods. It might be uncomfortable at the beginning, but we know it will benefit the students. As time progresses, we will become more comfortable with the change. In essence, we are moving from the shallow end to the deep end of the swimming pool.

Method vs. Message

While the message of education hasn't changed much over the years, the methods in which we present the message certainly have. For the most part, we're teaching the same reading, writing, and arithmetic skills our parents and grandparents were taught decades ago. But new instructional methods now exist (think: new math!) that previous generations did not have.

When I was in third grade, our teacher connected us with pen pals, which meant that we had to physically "pen" a letter and mail it to our "pal." Many of these pen pals were residents of a local nursing home in our town.

Today, students can log into Zoom or use FaceTime to communicate with students across the nation and from other countries, with just the click of a button. These are experiences our students will never forget.

In order to be relevant, we must be willing to adapt our methods with the technological updates of our day. We benefit because we learn the new skills necessary to make the experience happen; our students benefit because they reap the rewards of having the experience.

Invariably, there will be that one teacher who refuses to change, primarily because the idea wasn't their own. We can't let the thought of what *that* teacher or any other colleague might say stop us from trying new and innovative ideas. As with anything new, skeptics will always exist. It becomes our responsibility to work past them and create the experiences our students deserve.

While I was teaching, I was challenged by another teacher to create a "100 Point Club," celebrating students who earned a perfect 100% on any test throughout the year. I kept a running list of names on the board and promised pizza at the end of each quarter for those who earned the recognition. I found the idea to be elementary in nature, but I was floored with the response from my high school students!

My students loved that I was trying a new incentive program in the classroom. They held me accountable for making sure their names were added as I graded their tests. Students would double check every day to make sure their names were still on the board. It gave them a sense of pride. I noticed that even students who often earned B's started pushing themselves to earn A's. It was refreshing to see my students working so hard!

While we strive to stay relevant in the classroom, we must not forget that what we do today will have a lasting impact on our students. We already know that education uses a scaffolding approach, and our students learn one layer at a time. When we create a disconnect or refuse to adapt to what we should be doing, we thwart the opportunity for our students to grow.

TECHNOLOGY IS HERE TO STAY: LEARN TO EMBRACE IT

Our mathematics teacher always assigns a project which requires students to ask adults how they use mathematics in their everyday lives. I love his approach, because I remember being in high school and asking my teacher, "Am I going to use this in real life?"

I began to think about the last time I used the fundamentals of math in my daily life and pondered these questions:

- *When was the last time I balanced my checkbook?*
- *When was the last time I averaged grades with a calculator?*
- *When was the last time I used cash to pay for groceries or gas?*
- *When was the last time I mailed a check for my cable bill?*

I honestly answered, "I don't remember" or "It's been too long to remember" to most of these scenarios because technology has replaced each of these practices. I no longer have to manually balance my checkbook because my banking app does it automatically. I no longer have to average student grades because the online gradebook does it automatically. I no longer have to count out cash at the grocery store because I use my debit card. I no longer have to write out a check for any of my bills because I can pay them all online.

I often hear teachers say that we are "dumbing down" a generation of students because they don't understand how to conduct real research in a library. I cringe at these types of statements because they show how closed-minded we can become.

Apps like Siri and Google have replaced the need to read a newspaper, look through a phone book, or take a trip to the local library. I can ask Siri what the temperature is in my area and receive an immediate response. I can google directions or search for information about a topic and receive an instant list of websites and data. This has become a modern practice, not just in our daily lives, but in our classrooms as well.

We need to remember that technology shouldn't replace human connection. We have many opportunities to create experiences for students that will turn into memories. At our school, when our senior class votes on their annual senior trip destination, I always remind them that the location doesn't matter, it's the memories they create that matter.

The creativity of the instruction we provide for our students will ultimately drive what our students remember. It is not the technology itself we want them to remember; we want them to remember the experience of learning that the technology empowered.

FOLLOW-UP QUESTIONS:
CHAPTER TWELVE

1. Knowing that students today were born with technology at their disposal, how can you integrate technology into the classroom in a manner that is relevant?

2. How can you enhance your ability to adapt to ever-changing technology? How can you become more proficient at incorporating technology into your educational practices?

3. What are some ways you can merge traditional direct instruction with innovative strategies, such as a flipped-classroom model? Is this even possible?

4. I challenge you to find a Professional Learning Community in the social media sphere and make a connection with other educators. I am sure you will find that they are just as eager to share ideas and grow as you are.

Chapter Thirteen

Simple Math: You + Them & Conversation > Consequence

W hen I was in high school, one of my teachers was anxiously preparing for his annual in-classroom evaluation the next day. He was nervous about it and wanted to make a good showing, so he came up with a plan.

"Tomorrow," he said, "when I ask a question, raise your right hand if you know the correct answer. Raise your left hand if you don't know the correct answer. I will only call on you if you have your right hand raised. This will make me look good in front of the principal. It will look like all my students are paying attention and know the correct answers." Our class thought it was comical, so we played along the next day. I never found out, but I hope he got a complimentary review!

I remember nervously preparing myself for my first official evaluation by making sure every single category of the rating system my principal was going to be using was adequately covered. I wanted to make sure that I was providing quality instruction, and that my students were learning. At the same time, I was also making sure the components of my lesson plan were just perfect, my classroom management plan was accessible for review, and that I was integrating sufficient technology into my instruction. It was quite the challenge.

A few years into teaching, I began to understand that I needed to have a different mindset when it came to annual evaluations. I didn't want my principal to think I didn't measure up to his standards. I was so nervous about the evaluation that I was forgetting *why* I was being evaluated. Instead of being offended by the evaluation or comments, I decided to use these metrics in a positive way. I saw that I could use them as an aid to my professional development, as well as for the betterment of my students.

It's easy to make excuses during the evaluation process. I have learned, though, as a principal, excuses are usually a disguise for the unwillingness to do something or the reluctance to change a methodology to accommodate the needs of the students. We must not settle in a place of mediocrity and complacency. We must be willing to be stretched so that we can grow into and beyond what our evaluators and administrators desire for us.

LEADING BY LISTENING

We've all heard the adage: being born with two ears and one mouth means that we should listen twice as much as we speak. One way we can be stretched is by learning to listen. Whether it's listening to the professional feedback of administrators, listening to a student express their thoughts about a topic, or even listening to a parent vent their frustration about the quantity of homework that had been assigned the night before, we must pause and listen before responding. Sometimes, we have to listen to what is *really* being said and not to what the emotionalism of the moment makes us *think* is being said.

Learning from my classroom evaluations was beneficial; learning to listen to students and parents was invaluable. Taking the time to listen attentively to a parent, especially when they are upset about something that happened at school with their child, can pay great dividends for the student.

For example, I once encountered a parent who was demanding to meet with me because she was upset about the way the English teacher had graded her daughter's assignment. I read through the assignment and thought the student did a sufficient job, but then I read the grading rubric which noted that if the assignment responses weren't typed, students would only earn half the points possible.

When I pointed out to the mother that her daughter had not typed her assignment, she became enraged. She let me know that she was of the opinion that we should be more focused on the content—and not the appearance—of the work.

Knowing that our school's mission was to prepare students for college, I knew this simply wasn't practical. As we continued to talk, I found out that the real issue was that the family did not have a computer at home. When the mother finally calmed down, we were able to discuss how we could provide a way for her daughter to type and print her assignments before they were due.

Often, when we receive critical emails or texts from parents or colleagues, our first reaction is to reciprocate in the same way. To prevent this, I've often found myself opening a blank Word document and typing out my response before I send it. There is great benefit in composing our thoughts and making sure we are thinking with reason before responding out of emotion. If I receive an email like this on a Friday, I always wait until Monday to respond, as that ordinarily provides enough time for both parties to develop more rational thoughts.

When it comes to resolving issues with our students, determining why they are acting as they are is key. We sometimes reach our breaking point when students continually disrupt our lessons or after we've repeatedly attempted to redirect their behavior. Whenever I have made swift discipline decisions in these moments, it almost always leads to regret. Disciplining students while in an emotional state of frustration will often yield a negative response. Consequences should always equal, and not exceed, the level of the offense.

If students are continually acting out, it's an indication they are trying to tell us something—which means we should listen more intently. If our response comes from a place of frustration, we may even end up wanting to prove to the student (in front of the entire class) that their behavior will not be tolerated. Creating that type of atmosphere in the classroom will only serve to undermine what it is we are trying to accomplish in the lives of our students.

Some students crave being noticed, which is why they will continue to act out after being disciplined, simply because all the attention quickly shifts to them. It is important for us as educators to provide acknowledgment or affirmation to all of our students in a way that brings them confidence and lets them know that they matter.

Imagine what we could accomplish in the classroom if we became more intentional about making sure our students had an outlet to express themselves through their words or actions. Even better, imagine what our students would learn if we were to embed opportunities for that expression in our lessons and assignments.

We measure student success with a letter grade, but we must not forget to place value on student progress. We can think of progress as a garden with paving stones laid from one side to the other: if *success* means a student must move from one side of the garden to the other by the end of the unit, *progress* means that we are working to help the student move from one stone to the next, which will lead to success.

Too often, we seek success by skipping every other paving stone or skipping over content that might be too challenging, too time-consuming, or too frustrating. That very content might be what helps a student achieve mastery of an area in which they've always struggled.

We also shouldn't be afraid to allow students to express their creativity by sharing what they've learned.

Allowing students to express what they've learned in their own learning style will allow the student to function at their highest potential.

We might be amazed at what our students could accomplish if we were to take the time to talk with them individually and figure out how to meet their needs. I've often encountered students over the years who missed earning a passing grade on a test or in a class simply because they were absent during a unit or because they weren't paying attention and didn't turn in their homework. Closing these gaps requires extra time on our part, but it creates a connect-the-dots with the content which helps our students achieve mastery.

When we become intentional about not teaching to the "masses" but making sure we are meeting individual needs—even if it means providing extended time to complete an assignment, or offering tutoring for students who talked through our lesson the day before—it shows that we care about their individual success. We can't forget that students are just that: students.

They come to us from varied backgrounds and ability levels, and we must figure out what we can do to help every student become their best. We should never take their behavior personally, but we should always take it seriously.

We must learn to listen with the intent to understand, not with the intent to respond. When I first began to receive student office referral slips from teachers, I would begin my meetings with the students involved by saying, "Explain to me why you did this," which automatically put the student in the position of guilt. It wasn't until later that I learned that my words served to create a wall or a divide between me and the student.

There can be times when the summary written by the teacher isn't the full picture of an incident. In those cases, I might need to interview other students or even meet with the teacher for additional information. The intent is always to support the teacher; but as the principal, I also have to ensure that I'm making the best decision for the student. My desire is to capitalize on every opportunity to create a learning moment.

Now, I begin my meetings with students by saying, "Explain to me what happened." This eases the tension in my office, and it shows the student that I'm not being antagonistic toward them. At this point, the consequences could sway in any direction. This approach helps build trust with the student. I'm able to probe further with my questioning and try to get to the real root of the problem. In many cases, the action of the student was the outcome of an unresolved issue.

As educators, we must seek to understand why students act as they do. The problem might have been that the student was hungry, the student was being bullied by another student, or the student was simply intimidated by the teacher. Maybe the student was so far behind academically that he didn't know how to ask for help and sought attention in all the wrong ways.

When dealing with difficult situations involving students, I always use the following formula:

CONVERSATION > CONSEQUENCES

Taking the time to delve deeper into conversation with students will have a more meaningful outcome than simply assigning a consequence and sending the student back to class. *Both* a conversation and a consequence are often what is necessary to effectively reach a student. While students should not have to deal with adult-level issues, such as showing up to school without lunch money, they should be held accountable for their actions. The goal behind this concept is to move the student away from poor behavior and get them to understand—through conversation—the benefits of making better choices in the classroom and beyond.

I was recently conducting a prospective teacher interview, and asked one of the teachers on our staff to join me. As we were discussing potential student discipline issues, this teacher shared that whenever she needed to redirect students in her classroom, she would physically position herself on the same level as the student and then begin her conversation.

When implemented, this action will show the student that we want to help them, and not simply overpower them. This shows that we care, and that the conversation we're going to have is important. Another benefit of moving to their level is that both student and teacher can see and hear each other. This was a valuable concept to pass on to a new teacher.

When I meet with first-year teachers, I encourage them to try to maintain the same high level of excitement and anticipation throughout the year that they experienced before and on the first day of school.

If we think back to when we started teaching, we can remember how excited we were to finally end up in our own classroom. How many of us spent the majority of that summer creating lessons and designing units, meeting our colleagues and team teachers, and stocking up on an unorthodox amount of index cards and highlighters?

How many of us stayed at the school late the night before school began prepping our classroom and making sure everything was just right for the morning? How many of us laid out our clothes, packed our lunches, and set our alarms in anticipation of arriving on time for the first day of school? Imagine the benefit to our students if we were to maintain that energy every day and arrive prepared to take them on an educational journey that could change their lives forever!

One essential word of advice I share with new teachers is to make sure they understand that the success of the entire school year will be determined by their first interaction with the students. While in most cases this interaction will involve some type of icebreaker or "get-to-know-you" activity, it's also important to factor the need to structure and maintain classroom control and management.

I was working with a first-year teacher a few years ago on creating goals to help her strengthen her classroom management. My first priority was to help her understand the benefit of building positive relationships with her students. When I first introduce this idea to teachers, there are normally two streams of thought:

#1: I'm the teacher, you're the student, so do what I say. If you don't listen to my instruction, you are being insubordinate, I will be assigning discipline.

#2: I'm the teacher, you're the student, so let me figure out the best way to educate you. If you aren't initially receptive to my instruction, I need to figure out a different way to reach you.

In the course of our meeting, the teacher was expressing concerns about the poor behavior of the students in her class: "The 8th grade girls are getting progressively worse" and "Some of the rougher boys just don't show me any respect."

It was evident that there was a problem. Some of the students we were discussing were honor roll students with no behavior infractions other than the incident reports that she turned into the office.

I also learned from the students that she made comments which further created a divide between them. A few weeks earlier, she had been trying to get the attention of the students on the school bus during a field trip. Some of the students in the back of the bus were singing loudly and couldn't initially hear her. She shouted, "Be quiet! You are the worst students I've ever encountered!"

Her words told the students how she felt about them, which I quickly discovered was the root of her classroom management issues that year. Simply put, she had not developed any relationships with her students, nor did she want to take the time to make this a priority.

This teacher didn't realize it then, but she was implementing the following formula:

YOU (TEACHER) VS. THEM (STUDENTS)

The term "vs" or versus indicates a competition. There should never be a competition in education, especially between teacher and student. In a competition, both teams look for ways to win. The teacher more than likely will use office referrals as their weapon of choice, whereas the student has no choice other than to act out and use words or physical behavior as a means to defend and protect themselves. Trust me, I get it: in a perfect world, the student will respond with respect, and the parent will support us regarding any discipline.

We must understand that teaching is a service industry, whether we realize it or not. In education, our students are our customers. It's our responsibility to provide them with the best possible educational experience and to help them grow and develop into productive students and citizens. In order for us to accomplish this mission, we must continually seek new and innovative ways in which we can build trust and add to their growth. Think of teaching using this formula:

YOU (TEACHER) + THEM (STUDENTS)

In this formula, the symbol is a plus sign, which, as we know in mathematical terms, means addition. To find true success, we have to look for ways to add to the development of our students, rather than to subtract or divide. In the previous example about the students on the field trip, the teacher created a divide between herself and the students, which led to a catastrophic year for both parties.

One solution I shared with the teacher was that she could have simply moved to the back of the bus to figure out why the students were making so much noise. She would have noticed that the students had their headphones in and couldn't hear her.

Asking those students to remove their headphones would have been much more beneficial than losing her cool and shouting at the group of students as a whole. As a follow-up, she could have provided an avenue within some of her future lessons that allowed students to express themselves through song, while making sure they were following the established rules and procedures.

When we allow students to express themselves and share from their viewpoint or level of experience, we are providing opportunities for them to step up and become leaders in the classroom. I have always been amazed at what students can accomplish when I simply move to the back seat and let them take control of elements within their education. The formula now looks like this:

ROLE REVERSAL: THEM (STUDENTS) + YOU (TEACHERS)

I'm reminded of one of my former students named Elijah. Elijah was a strong leader among his peers, by both guiding and encouraging students to make right decisions, and by the value he placed on his own character, integrity, and personal growth. He was elected student body president in his senior year and graduated as the valedictorian. He was offered nearly $500,000 in college scholarships as a result of his hard work and academic achievement.

During his senior year, Elijah submitted a proposal to me for a program he wanted to implement called PREP groups. PREP was an acronym that stood for Positivity, Responsibility, Elevation, and Preparation. His proposal called for splitting up the student body into separate advisory groups with one faculty advisor to oversee each group. The groups would meet every other week on Friday afternoons. Elijah and the senior student council officers created a curriculum, complete with character training activities and group discussion points.

The focus of each group meeting was to provide students with the opportunity to share some of the positive things taking place in their lives, to encourage students to learn the value of responsibility in their school performance, to praise students for achieving their goals, and to help prepare students academically and socially for their next grade level.

I asked Elijah to introduce the PREP groups concept at a faculty meeting and share his vision for the program. The reason I approved the program and allowed Elijah to implement it at our school was because I believed in his leadership abilities. I knew he was capable of positively impacting many students, which could shift the culture of the school.

I also wanted to add to his leadership development. His reputation preceded him, and I knew that if he were provided with the opportunity to exceed the standard, he would do everything in his power to do so. I knew that in an initiative like this, the growth had to be organic and needed to be presented from the bottom up (students to the teachers), not from the top down (teachers to the students).

It took some time for all the teachers to catch the vision of the PREP groups. I've learned that even though students might not think something is "cool," if we give them an opportunity to do something other than fill in a worksheet or take notes, they will usually support it. Students eventually engaged in intriguing discussions involving teenage issues and daily struggles. They even participated in leadership training exercises and activities.

One day, all the students wore name tags labeled with the trait for which they wanted to be known. This was not only a way to encourage them on their journey, but also to allow students to keep each other accountable for their words and deeds. I attribute the success of the implementation to Elijah and his council of student officers.

After graduation, Elijah went on to attend college. There, he was elected to the campus student council as a freshman, and was also elected president of the international student council. While in college, he held a part-time job at a pizza restaurant in central Ohio. The restaurant chain operated nearly 200 locations, and he moved up quickly through the ranks as a shift manager at his location.

He valued leadership to the point that he arranged to meet with the chairwoman of the board and the founder of the company to learn more about the business principles that had brought the company nearly $200 million in sales the previous year. The chairwoman and the founder might not have realized it at the time, but they, too, were adding to Elijah's growth—not only in his personal life, but also in his professional life, which would ultimately help their company.

Students often mirror our behavior, and we must care enough to make the right choices in our actions and words. Thankfully, Elijah found role models within his educational setting who believed in him and encouraged him, who were able to add to him.

But what happens if things don't seem to be turning out as well? What happens if we make mistakes and decisions that negatively affect a student? When those moments occur, we need to find the strength to apologize or to correct the decision, and to do so humbly. Relationships often start with a simple conversation, and sometimes cost us our pride. We must do what is right, not what is easy. We must understand that when we subtract from a student, we stunt their growth and potential.

This principle can be applied to other groups of people, not just to our students. We can also look for ways that we can add to the parents of our students and to our colleagues at the school. We can seek out ways to add to the individual people in our personal lives. These people might be our spouses, our children, our neighbors, our colleagues, or our friends. Who knows what might happen as a result of taking the time to care about them and their lives? If this is the mindset we maintain, there is no need to be nervous about a teacher evaluation—our desire to provide a rewarding educational experience for our students will shine through!

FOLLOW-UP QUESTIONS:
CHAPTER THIRTEEN

1. What is one strategy you can begin to implement when you feel offended by a comment on your annual teaching evaluation?

2. Under what circumstances would it be appropriate to allow students to express their thoughts and emotions?

3. Which do you feel is more important: success or progress? Why?

4. Can you describe a scenario in which a consequence might be more effective than a conversation?

Chapter Fourteen

Parents, Educators, Students: Moving in the Same Direction

W hen I graduated from high school, I enlisted in the United States Air Force, where I served as an aircraft mechanic for the duration of my enlistment. On many of my shifts, I had to troubleshoot airplanes that were decades old and that weren't equipped with the state-of-the-art technology found in most military airplanes today.

I had to figure out what wasn't operating properly and which components needed to be repaired or replaced, often spending many hours on the flight-line troubleshooting parts. In order for the airplane to fly safely and accomplish each mission, all the parts had to function correctly, both independently and concurrently.

As educators, we often have to do the same thing in the classroom in order to meet the needs of our students. We will inevitably encounter situations with students, parents, or even colleagues that will force us to think both analytically and innovatively in order to find resolution or compromise.

Just because a strategy works for one situation doesn't mean it will work for another. We must remember, especially when it comes to our students, that no amount of troubleshooting is too much. We must do whatever it takes to meet their needs in the classroom.

The educational process is made up of three distinct components which function together like gears, each with its own level of responsibility and accountability. These gears must turn in the same direction and fit together and operate in unity in order for there to be a successful outcome. These three gears in the educational process are the parents, the educators, and the students.

GEAR #1: THE PARENTS

In most cases, the parents are going to be the biggest advocates and "experts" on the topic of their child. A child often spends more time with their parents than with any other adult. Until the child goes to daycare or preschool, the main adult or teacher in the child's life is usually a parent.

Parents know their child's favorite food and their child's favorite color. They were there for their child's first steps, the first time they learned to ride a bicycle, and for their first day of school. They know any injuries their child has sustained, they know their child's favorite superhero, and they know the names of their child's playmates and friends. They know what triggers their child to respond to certain situations, and they know their child's strengths and weaknesses.

It is natural, normal, and understandable for parents to be possessive and protective of their child. We should not only understand this as educators, but we should anticipate it. We often see situations like this in the classroom, especially if the child is the first or the only child in their family. Not only is the schooling process a first experience for the child, it's also the first experience for the parents to function as parents of a child in school.

Parents all function at many levels. Some are extremely involved, some are moderately involved, and others have little or no involvement except for what is absolutely required by law. We should also keep in mind that in many situations, grandparents, aunts and uncles, and other relatives or family friends are fulfilling the parental role for a student.

When it comes to our role as educators, we must seek to build a bridge with parents in order to develop a partnership. There will be many times when a student will need to work on assignments at home or even by staying late in the classroom. We will need to create an open dialogue with parents. This dialogue is also important in the event any issues arise with the student in the course of the school year.

If we are having issues with a student in our classroom, we should first speak to the student, and if the issues continue, contact the parents next. When engaging in conversation with a parent, the "compliment sandwich" method is helpful. In this approach, the conversation begins with a compliment about something the student has recently achieved, then gets into the meat of the conversation or the issue, then closes with a compliment directed toward the parent.

I'm telling on myself here, but I once had a situation with a student that left me perplexed. The student was in middle school and seemed to have a chip on her shoulder. She appeared to always have a scowl on her face, and she just didn't seem to be a fan of teachers—or any adults—for that matter.

Her brother happened to be one of our student office helpers that year during one of his free periods. I had a good rapport with him, so one day I asked him in casual conversation what I could do to help his sister. My intention was to figure out how to best help her while she was at the school.

Fast forward a few weeks. I had a conference with the parents of the student, and it came up that I had spoken with the brother about the sister. I mentioned that I didn't want to worry the parents about something that seemed trivial. The parents didn't receive that information very well. They became upset, and frankly, had every right to be. They made it known that if there were ever any issue with one of their children, my first step should be to contact them, not their other child.

Looking back, I realize I should have contacted them directly. In the moment, I had seen no harm in talking to the brother, but I now realize the value of establishing that relationship and dialogue directly with the parents.

Building this bridge with the parents helps in many ways. When we establish trust with the parents, they will more fully embrace us educators and will be assured we have their child's best interest in mind. These same parents will often be the ones who will volunteer as chaperones for a field trip or as room parents to help with a holiday party. They will be more likely to support us on our quest to create memorable and meaningful learning experiences for their child.

GEAR #2: THE EDUCATORS

Let's look at the function of an educator. We know that our goal as educators is to inspire our students through our instruction. We use a myriad of ways to do so, integrating various curriculum elements such as technology, experiences, and field trips. We work hard at making sure we have a full understanding of our content area, and we attend as many professional development workshops as we can.

We spend time during the summer prepping for the next school year by searching online for the newest classroom fads and instructional models. We put pleas on our social media accounts for our friends to donate extra chairs and couches so that our students could enjoy the ever-popular flexible seating arrangement.

We often spend entirely too much money on bulletin board borders and plastic organizational containers. Our classroom closets are already full of left-over boxes of tissues and hand sanitizer from the previous year, but we can never have too much, right?

We take an immense amount of pride in our profession. We strive to create ideal lessons that encompass the diverse types of students and learners in our classrooms. We want to make sure all our students enjoy the experiences we create for them.

Even if our efforts and energy seem to go unnoticed or unappreciated, we should understand that when it comes to parents, they too, are working hard to make sure their child has their needs met and is put in a position to succeed.

We must show respect for the work parents do during the hours their child isn't at school. They're the ones who are helping our students with their homework assignments and projects. They're the ones working all day to provide meals and shelter each night. As much as we want parents to support *us*, we should seek ways to show parents that we support *them*.

Educators often serve as another set of "parents." We often have to figure out creative ways to meet non-academic needs, too. Students will remember how they are treated, and they will never forget how an adult makes them feel. We should create classroom environments that demonstrate love and safety. Students should authentically feel loved and safe, just as if they were at home.

Consistency is key when involving parents in education. Making sure we communicate with parents daily or weekly by providing updates about lesson plans and homework is vital, as is always informing parents of upcoming due dates or the dates for other activities and events. Communicating in a professional way shows the passion and desire we have to help their child succeed.

We should also be quick to communicate milestones and successes in the classroom with parents. If a student works hard on a project and earns a high grade, email the parents! If a student finally has a breakthrough and scores well on a state standardized test, let mom or dad know! If a student who always seems to disregard school or classroom rules has a really great day or week, call home at the end of the day, before the student even gets off the bus!

Imagine how that student will feel walking through the door and having mom or dad beam with pride knowing that their child finally achieved compliance with the expectation. Small accomplishments are still accomplishments. All accomplishments deserve to be celebrated, no matter how seemingly insignificant.

GEAR #3: THE STUDENTS

Now, let's look at the student. To put it in simplest terms, it's the student's responsibility to show up at school and learn. In a perfect world, our entire classroom of students would show up with zeal and energy and have a passion for learning. They would all come to school with their homework completed and ask for their next assignments.

They would also ask for rigorous content and look at how what they're learning plays into the comprehensive canvas of their education. They would understand the benefits of studying hard for tests, and the value of working with a partner, and the profit in group discussions. They would feel the passion their teacher has and transfer that energy into their effort in the classroom work ethic.

Don't get me wrong, there are students who mirror this description. But there are also students who both on paper and in person completely contradict this description, even when we feel like we have given our all through our lessons. When we understand our students as individuals, we are then able to ascertain a better understanding of what is required to educate each one of them.

When I taught high school history, I jokingly asked my students once when they were grumbling about a research assignment if any of them were sweating. I knew they weren't because our building was new and had air conditioning. Puzzled, they looked at me and responded with, "No."

One student even mumbled under his breath, "I think the man has lost his mind, because it's like 68 degrees in here!" I continued by telling them that sweat comes after effort.

I thought it was a pretty profound way to motivate my students to work harder at completing the assignment, until one of my students asked, "Mr. Mills, why aren't you sweating? It looks like you need to work harder, too!"

He was right. I knew that I couldn't just give them an assignment and see what they would accomplish. I needed to work alongside them through the process and engage them in authentic learning.

His statement encouraged me to work with my students for the duration of their research project. I didn't just leave the responsibility in their hands. I decided that instead of listening to them complain, I would show them by modeling the effort of what it looks like to conduct research.

These are the types of moments that enable us to build relationships with our students and through which they are able to learn. There is no greater learning experience than in the one-on-one setting. Foundational learning is still learning.

Students should be encouraged to ask questions if they need help with something—chances are, they are not the only one in the room with the same question. Imagine if we reteach a seemingly simple concept or reiterate a seemingly simply procedure, how many more students might move farther ahead simply by that one planned or unplanned adjustment in the lesson.

If we have to show students how to format a research paper when they are in 12th grade, then we show them. This might be the last opportunity they will have to learn the keys to success that they will need when they step foot on the university campus the next fall or when they enter the work force and are tasked with new responsibilities.

We are often too quick to assume that students know how to do something, when, in reality, we need to take the time to teach them.

An example of this was the time I was teaching a lesson about the American presidents. Because I knew our school's curriculum, I just assumed that my students had background knowledge of the major presidencies in our nation's history. I failed to remember that much like any subject, review is necessary and needed.

About half-way through the lesson, the need for review became apparent! At that point, I integrated a historical timeline activity to help my students freshen up on their knowledge of history. As a result, the rest of the main lesson was much easier to teach and more students were able to attain mastery of the subject.

Throughout my career as both a teacher and an administrator, I have observed that when parents, educators, and students work together as a team, the "gears" of education function much more smoothly: parents have more confidence in their child's school, educators are more fulfilled in their respective roles, and more students have better educational outcomes.

A AND B

Educational partnership is not conditional. A conditional statement reads, "If a parent or student does A, then the teacher will do B." Our partnership is nonconditional; we have to come to school each day prepared to do both A and B.

If the student or parent skips A, it might mean that the student will fail the assignment or be robbed of the opportunity for learning. It is our job to step in and close the gap. Our willingness and motivation to help our students is not predicated on what they or their parents do or don't do, it is predicated on who we are: educators.

It certainly helps us when parents strive to ensure that the student has their homework completed and when the student comes to school prepared and ready to learn. Our goal should be to move the student in the right direction, regardless of the level of support received outside of the school.

Then there are the times when parents will try to do both A and B for the student. We call these types of parents "helicopter" parents, in that they hover over their child to make sure they are doing what they're supposed to be doing. Now, there is a new group of parents called "snowplow" parents, who like a plow, go before their child to ensure there isn't any difficulty or challenge that their student won't be able to handle.

I recognize that sometimes it takes longer for the student to find success through independence, and that's perfectly okay. It's unreasonable to place an unspoken demand on a student that they should know how to execute a task before a certain age or grade level. We sometimes aren't privy to the home life or to the academic background of the child, so it's understandable that parents often want to be fully immersed in their child's development.

Both educators and parents should endeavor to motivate and inspire the student. As a school principal, I'm now learning the value of integrating all types of parents into the school environment. We all long for acceptance and personal connection, and parents are no exception. When we take the time to discover their strengths and talents, we are then able to use those strengths in ways that will better advance our classrooms and schools.

We must work together and keep the student at the core of every decision that is made. When we encounter situations where we just can't make progress with a parent, it might simply be a personality clash. In situations like these, we treat that parent the same as we would any other parent, by continuing to communicate in a professional way.

A person will do more and be more cooperative when they feel appreciated. We can begin developing our relationship with parents by complimenting them and acknowledging the work they do in the raising of their child. At the end of the day, regardless of how much effort it takes to move the gears forward with parents and students, it is important to remember we are not striving for perfection, we are striving for progress.

FOLLOW-UP QUESTIONS: CHAPTER FOURTEEN

1. What does "troubleshooting" look like inside the classroom?

2. Is it ever appropriate to let a student know you disagree with their parents?

3. How do you communicate with a parent when professionally you believe you have the best solution for their child, but they disagree with you?

Chapter Fifteen

Calculated Communication: Creating a Healthy Dialogue

I once heard a story about a person being sent on an errand to the local grocery store to purchase a few items. Here was the list:

One gallon of milk
One 12-pack of soda
One pound turkey

The person shopping went into the first store and couldn't find a one-pound turkey, so they ventured into two more grocery stores, with no luck in either.

When the shopper returned home, they informed the other relatives that they had been able to find everything on the list except the one-pound turkey. Everyone burst out laughing because the intention had been for the shopper to purchase one pound of turkey meat from the deli, not an actual turkey weighing one pound!

When we are communicating, we have to remember that it's not for our benefit, but it's for the benefit of the other person, or in our situation, our students. Each student will hear what we're saying and respond according to how they interpreted what we said.

I'm sure we've all encountered situations where parents were upset about something their child shared with them that had happened at school that day. In most cases, I don't believe students intentionally lie, but they might spin the story so that it benefits their intended goal.

One time, I had to deal with a parent who was upset with a teacher because her son supposedly hadn't been given enough time at school to complete his online math assignments. After conferencing with the teacher, I learned that the students had approximately 15 minutes in class to complete a few tasks.

They had been given an in-class assignment pertaining to the lesson that had been taught that day. Once they finished the assignment, they were to move directly to their online math modules. If the online math modules couldn't be completed at school, they were automatically assigned as homework for that night and would be due the next morning.

While some students finished everything in class, others had to finish it for homework. The student told his mother that the teacher didn't give him enough time in school to finish his online math, so therefore, he earned a poor grade. The parent was unaware that the assignment could also be completed at home and that it was required for homework, if not finished in school.

The student didn't lie, but only gave his mother enough information to protect himself from getting into trouble. Fortunately, the mother was understanding, and the student received another opportunity to complete the assignment.

INITIAL COMMUNICATION: BENEFITS TO REACHING OUT FIRST

It's imperative that educators communicate with parents within the first two weeks of school. This can be carried out through several different forms of communication. I've seen elementary teachers mail postcards to students before school starts, introducing themselves to the student and stating how excited they are to have that student in their class. I've also seen teachers mail individualized letters, with a self-addressed return envelope, asking the student to write an introductory letter about themselves and mail it back to the teacher. This example not only gets students involved in the writing process, but also teaches them how to address and mail a letter, which has slowly become a lost art.

Typically, the older the students, the less engaging this type of communication becomes. At the high school level, an email blitz to all our students and their parents will suffice. It's important to make contact and introduce ourselves, while also providing our classroom expectations and policies in writing. This will help us, especially if we encounter a behavior issue or an academic situation that requires parental involvement within the first few weeks. Since there was some form of introduction, the parent will at least know who we are and can refer to our communication, if necessary.

We often form an idea about someone based on the information we've picked up from other people—even if we don't really know the person or know their intentions. This is simply unfair to both the person and to us. That person should have the opportunity to explain their concerns, and we deserve the opportunity to build a relationship.

When we communicate, whether it's written or verbal, we need to make sure our communication is clear, direct, and understandable. When I was a teacher, one of my principals always encouraged the staff to keep our parent communication simple. He said directions should be clear enough for an 8th grade student to understand them. He wasn't trying to insult the level of intelligence among the parents; he was simply stating that if we're trying to communicate something important, we should keep it simple enough so that it can be easily understood by all.

The same is true with instruction in our classrooms. While the content itself should be grade- and course-level appropriate, the manner in which we teach and communicate that content should be clear and comprehensible to all levels of learners in our classroom. If our instruction and communication style is challenging to understand or follow, then the content itself will more than likely not be understood either.

Using humor and sarcasm in the classroom is a recipe for potential disaster. There is a difference between humor and sarcasm. What is funny to one person may not be funny to another. As I have learned the hard way, what is perceived as sarcastic by one might be perceived as offensive to another.

What we say will get back to us one way or another. It might be that a teacher overheard students talking about a joke we told or something we said in class, and they wanted to let us know that some students took offense to it. Or it might be a parent who expressed concerns over what their child told them we said in class. Again, while it might be a partial truth, we still have to provide justification for our words, especially if they weren't communicated in a professional or fair way.

When using humor, we need to work to make sure we are not being offensive to any students in our classroom. This means we have to make an effort to understand the demographic of our students: their ethnicities, race, socio-economic backgrounds, and at times, even their religious beliefs. We never want to tell a joke only to have it backfire and offend a student.

YOUR BODY LANGUAGE SAYS IT ALL

I had a teacher in high school who never stood up from her desk. She was probably 25 years into her career when I was in her class, and it was evident that she was doing the bare minimum—just punching the proverbial time clock until she was eligible for retirement. She wasn't very friendly, and she made trivial tasks overly complicated. Her class was the longest 40 minutes of my day.

Her body language showed me that she didn't care about us enough to at least stand up and teach. She didn't greet any of her students at the door, nor did she say goodbye as we left her classroom. To this day, I remember the experience she created, and it wasn't one I would wish on any of my students.

I'm not saying that we should have to get on top of our students' desks or dance around the classroom during our instruction, but we should be visible and accessible to all our students. Instead of having students come to our desk, we can create a system where we meet them in their learning spaces. This allows us to address our students quietly and appropriately, or answer the questions they have about the assignment.

We must also watch our facial expressions—our students can read them. Students know when we are genuinely excited to see them—our faces reflect this. Students can also sense when we become frustrated. When students sense their teacher is upset, it can trigger anxiety, especially in younger students. If the students are creating the frustration, we should respond sternly, but never out of a place of anger.

COMMUNICATION OUTSIDE OF THE CLASSROOM

We can show our students we care about them in more ways than just their academic development. Our actions will demonstrate to our students what we are trying to communicate to them. For example, when I get invited to events for my students outside of school, such as music performances, AAU basketball games, dance recitals, and the like, I do my best to attend and support them. When I am able to attend these events, I always look for the family of the student and make sure to connect with the parents of the student.

By engaging with my students and their families, I am demonstrating that what is important to them is important to me. When I receive an invitation to one these events, I'm always surprised to see their reactions when I actually show up!

One of my former students started a t-shirt clothing company with his brother. He invited all his friends through social media, but he sent me a text and invited me, hoping I would make it to the launch party. I did everything I could to ensure I was able to attend. This communicated to him that I believed in his dream enough to invest an hour of my day and to spend $20 on a t-shirt.

Last summer, an incoming freshman called me at the school. I didn't immediately recognize the number, but when I answered the phone, I heard, "Hey Mr. Mills, this is Paris. I don't want anything, but I just wanted to see how your summer is going." That phone call made my day. Paris told me that he had made the national track meet for his summer team, he was excited about taking a higher-level math course during the upcoming school year, and that he had been staying up late every night playing Fortnite with his friends.

By taking 10 minutes out of my day to talk with a student like Paris, not only was I cultivating the relationship, but through my communication, I was creating a level of trust that showed I cared about him. I wonder if I should start saving money now in case he asks me to attend his national track meet!

SOCIAL MEDIA SAFETY

Every school or district has policies concerning social media interaction with students. My school's policy is that staff and students are not permitted to become friends or follow each other on the various social media sites and apps. I do have parents who follow me, but I only accept friend requests from students once they have graduated.

The easiest way to avoid this issue is to create our own social media pages for our classrooms. This allows students, parents, and even grandparents to follow what we're doing. In addition to the school's parent portal, we can post assignments, reminders, test review questions, and pictures of projects. We can even highlight students who earned high scores on tests.

We can invite our principal and other teachers in our building to join the page, as it adds a built-in accountability for safety. We can serve as the moderator, blocking inappropriate content and ensuring that everything remains professional. We can monitor the page and prevent students or parents from venting their frustrations or posting comments that are contrary to the purpose of the page.

When it comes to our personal social media, we should always keep in mind that what we post on the

Internet will remain on the Internet, potentially forever, even if we delete it. More and more companies and schools are holding employees accountable for what they post on their personal social media accounts. My general rule is that if I would be embarrassed to see this on the local news with my name attached to it, I probably shouldn't post it.

It is wise to refrain from discussions about race, politics or other controversial subjects with current parents or colleagues on public platforms. This isn't to say that we do not have the first amendment freedom to share our thoughts and beliefs, but that we should be cognizant of who is "following" our pages and where our information could potentially end up.

COMMUNICATION: 24-HOUR RULE

We should also be aware that *no* communication is still communication. If a parent or a student reaches out to us through email or by leaving a phone message with the office, we need to respond. Not responding still sends a message, just not the right one.

I set up a policy in my school that teachers are mandated to respond to all parent communication within 24 hours of receiving it. They don't necessarily have to have the answer the parent is looking for in that time frame, but they have to at least acknowledge that the message has been received, and that they are working diligently on getting the requested information. Obviously, if the answer is something that can be provided right away, we should respond sooner.

When we don't respond to communication, or it takes us a week to respond to a simple email, it shows the parent that we aren't organized with our time, and that we don't value theirs. Weekends and holidays would be the only acceptable exception to the 24-hour policy. Teachers are allowed to rest, too! Those "out-of-office" auto responses work like magic, even if we're checking our email over a holiday break or long weekend. The auto responses don't lock us into an immediate required response.

If we are hesitant to return a phone call or email because of the nature of the communication sent by the parent, we can include our principal in our response. If the parent is upset or disagrees with a decision we made, we need to be certain that we have the appropriate justification for our decision and that we have communicated in a professional way. A phone call will often help clear up any miscommunication that was transmitted through email.

THERE'S NO ROOM FOR NEGATIVITY

It is never acceptable to speak negatively about another student, teacher, or parent in front of a student, teacher, or parent. We might be stuck on how to help a struggling learner, and if we're sharing that information with another teacher, it should be from the reference point of asking for feedback or suggestions. Complaining about the deficiencies of a student without seeking a solution doesn't solve the problem; it shows a lack of professionalism and care for the student.

It might be easy to join the conversation in the staff lounge about the principal or even a colleague who appears to be an easy target, but these discussions are in poor taste and will reflect negatively on our character.

Remember, every person has a person. We all have a friend with whom we share information. These friends have a friend, their friend might have a friend, and so on. It never fails that, at some point, the information we shared will get back to the person. Then, we have to spend time justifying and explaining ourselves. If we have an issue with someone, we should seek them out in a professional way and share our thoughts. The goal is to work cohesively with our colleagues.

As educators, we should band together. I'm not insinuating that education is an army of teachers defending ourselves against parents. However, we must protect and support each other when we have the opportunity to do so. If a parent is complaining about a teacher, encourage them to dig deeper into the issue and to schedule a meeting with that teacher.

Chiming into the conversation by agreeing with the parent about how poor the teacher's organization skills are or how unable they are to manage a classroom is simply unprofessional. It also is a poor reflection of our school, which we should be proud to represent.

Our communication is a reflection of who we are. Our goal should be to strive to make sure it's positive, efficient, and productive.

FOLLOW-UP QUESTIONS:
CHAPTER FIFTEEN

1. What are some ways you can ensure that your communication to parents and students is clear, concise, and to the point?

2. How do you respond when you reach out to a parent and they do not return your calls or emails? What do you do if you have important information you need to share with them?

3. Because teachers receive numerous invites from students for both school-sanctioned and out-of-school events, how can you graciously decline an invitation while still showing the student you care about them?

4. There are many "don'ts" when it comes to teachers and students becoming "friends" on social media. What are some websites or apps that are student-friendly and appropriate for use in the classroom?

Chapter Sixteen

Building a Culture of Care

"**W**ould I be learning if I were a student in my own classroom?" This is a question we must continually ask ourselves. There are going to be days when it's easier on us to just have our students read silently and answer questions on a worksheet instead of creating an innovative and technology-driven lesson.

Trust me, I get it—we've all been there. But we must remember it is our responsibility to create the culture of our classrooms and schools. If we don't establish the necessary culture on the first day of class, the students will. The tone will be set that they have free reign and you hold no authority.

It is up to us to make sure students understand classroom expectations: how they are to treat other students, how and when they can respond and speak, how and when they can interact with their phones and other technology. These are all factors that pertain to establishing an effective classroom culture. When we are putting culture into place, it should be for the benefit and well-being of our students.

DEFINING CULTURE

Just like every school has a culture, whether created intentionally or not, every classroom also has a culture. The culture of our classroom doesn't just focus on our management plan and discipline structure, it also focuses on the caliber of our instruction and the quality and equity of our interactions with our students.

The culture of our classroom sets the tone for the school year. It focuses on the big picture, yet it can be summarized briefly. It is succinct enough that someone else could easily describe our style and the type of classroom we lead—for instance:

"She's tough when it comes to grading."

"He always provides extra time for late work."

"We always have the opportunity to use technology."

One humbling way to assess the current climate of our classroom is to ask our students to anonymously write three adjectives that describe the classroom environment. We often view things one way, but sometimes the translation comes across as something completely different.

I'm not saying we should create a classroom culture based on student opinion, but understanding what they are saying helps us understand what they are feeling. Understanding how they feel is important, not because it's our reputation on the line, but because we care about their well-being. If students don't feel safe, if students don't feel the classroom is structured, and if students don't feel like they are learning, then changes have to be made, and they must be made sooner rather than later.

At no point should the feedback from our students ever be used against them. Their thoughts and feelings matter, and making the necessary changes to accommodate a level of care that takes their thoughts and feelings into consideration is truly valuable. That which is important to our students should become important to us, too.

As the teacher in the classroom, we know what our students need in order to become successful. Even if we do ask for the opinion of our students when creating culture, if they respond with statements such as, "We don't want any homework!" or "We should have more recess time!" we understand that while we might be able to integrate these suggestions occasionally, these types of suggestions will probably be disregarded.

When students share about how they feel or they express concerns with their learning, we should seek ways to integrate their suggestions. For instance, if a student says, "I don't understand the way Mr. Smith teaches math, and I feel like I'm falling behind now," and that student has a very low grade, it's imperative that changes be made in order to help that student learn.

Students should know and feel our culture from the time they enter the classroom until they leave. How students enter our classroom will determine the climate of our classroom. Establishing a routine by greeting students at the door, assigning bell work or morning work, making sure students know our expectations, and setting deadlines will create a system with which our students will become familiar.

Chaos will ensue if the routine changes every day. When students enter the classroom, they will not know what to expect or what to do. It's okay for the suspense of our instruction to keep the students on their toes, but there must be an established routine at the beginning and end of each class period, and during all transitions.

There is no greater struggle for a teacher than trying to settle a classroom of students after lunch or after recess. Having to yell, "Be quiet and sit down!" or "I'm going to stand here until you're quiet!" every single day—and it's only October—will make it an extremely long year! This is why students need to know and fully understand our routines from the moment they cross the threshold from the hallway and enter our classroom.

I encourage making students the priority during instruction by integrating their favorite things. If we really want to see students respond to us, we can use their verbiage, integrate lyrics from popular songs, or make references to superstar athletes. I've often found that when I do this, I become more of a joke, which I'm okay with, as it shows my human side. Students will appreciate our efforts, and they'll laugh every time we try to say something that ends up coming across as humorous.

For some of our students, we might be the only laugh they have that day, so it's definitely worth it. And I would almost guarantee that the students will talk about our shenanigans throughout the day and even share their experience with their parents when they get home, which is what we ultimately want.

GIVING VS. TAKING

I don't think any quality educator wants to see students fail an assignment or assessment. At the same time, I don't think there is any benefit to giving students grades for simply showing up. I always stress the importance of assigning grades for academic purposes only. Students shouldn't be awarded points for a binder check or for having basic supplies. These types of checks should be rewarded based on our enrichment or incentive programs, whether it be individual or team points, extra recess, or some type of candy or treat.

I do believe there is a benefit in establishing a system that allows students multiple attempts to master a concept. Why is it that students can write a rough draft, a first draft, and a second draft when writing a research paper? Or why are there multiple steps and often multiple tries when it comes to the scientific method and experiments in science class, but with mathematics and social studies, students often have only one opportunity to correctly answer a question?

Instead of taking away, we should seek to give. Providing students with the opportunity to earn partial points for correcting missed test questions not only gives the student a chance to raise their grade, but it also helps students improve their understanding of the content. Placing a requirement for effort behind the additional points provides the necessary justification for raising their grade.

I once read about a teacher who created all her tests in the likeness of the game show, *Who Wants to be a Millionaire* and allowed students to use "lifelines." These ranged from asking a friend for a hint, having one minute to review their notes (during the test), and even asking for a hint from the teacher. This creativity allowed for students to refresh themselves on content that might have slipped their minds. Nothing is worse than when a student says, "Man, I knew that!" as they look at their study guide after they turned in the test.

It would be great if every student in the classroom finished the quarter with an A—if they earned it. One of my former colleagues, now retired, taught chemistry. Mrs. Watkins was a very tough teacher and students often initially struggled in her class. However, she was also the team statistician for our school's volleyball program, so she would stay after school until the games started. She made this time available to students so they could stay and receive individualized tutoring.

Mrs. Watkins wasn't just going to help a student; she was going to sit with that student and not let them leave the tutoring session until they fully understood the material. She was one of those teachers whom the students could look back on and think, "Wow, she certainly prepared me for college." This was the culture she established, and she did so with a tremendous level of care and consideration for her students.

All roads should lead to learning. While we often want to teach our students lessons about responsibility, our focus needs to be on teaching them lessons about the content we are qualified and licensed to teach. All elements of our instruction should be strategic. It's as if our students are putting together an academic puzzle. Every element should be a piece that fits into the whole. They should be able to look back at the end of a lesson, a lab, or even after submitting a research paper, and be amazed at how much they learned during the process.

THE PHYSIOLOGICAL FACTOR

I've mentioned this already, but I believe it's worth repeating: the key differentiating factor between a teacher and an educator is that the educator takes care of the physiological needs of the student, in addition to their academic needs. I'm referring to provisionary needs such as food, clothing, and hygiene products.

While these items cost money, there are ways in which we can collect donations from our family and friends, and even solicit help through social media. Department stores, churches, and other non-profit agencies in the area might be willing to donate supplies and help keep items stocked for the students.

Basic items can include toothbrushes and toothpaste, deodorant, crackers, granola bars and other snacks that students can take home to eat later that night or even for breakfast if the school doesn't have a breakfast program. Some schools have created a "Community Closet" where students can wash their clothes during the school day and even pick out donated clothing items to wear. Another need that could be met would be to stock basic school supply items. In addition to educators spending their own money, some PTO organizations might support the initiative if asked.

We can ask teachers to have students turn in extra supplies at the end of the school year. We can ask parents to consider purchasing a few extra items for the community supply shelf for students in need when they're shopping for school supplies in August, especially during the back-to-school tax-free weekend!

I firmly believe that when we take care of the student, our subject area and our classroom management will all take care of themselves. We shouldn't make provision available for students to expect them to behave and treat us better; we should make provision available for students because we genuinely care about them.

When we are engaging with a student in need, we need to do so in private and not in a way that will embarrass the student. Drawing undue attention to the student in the middle of a silent reading activity—where every student is going to look up from their reading if we reach into the supply drawer and hand the student a toothbrush and toothpaste—would not be the best approach! We will need to think creatively, but that creativity will show the student how much we care.

When students can both see and know that we care, that is when we are making a difference. That is when we are making an impact. Making an impact doesn't start school-wide or district-wide; it starts by connecting with that one student. Who is that student for you?

FOLLOW-UP QUESTIONS: CHAPTER SIXTEEN

1. While it's important to establish classroom expectations on the first day of school, why is the second day of school even more important?

2. How would you define the culture of your classroom? Are there elements or policies you could change that would help students thrive?

3. What is your philosophy when it comes to grading and giving students more than one attempt to correctly answer questions? Does your philosophy help students achieve mastery?

4. What are some creative ways you can motivate other teachers and staff in your building to join you in creating a culture of care to meet these often basic and overlooked needs of students?

Chapter Seventeen

Right Voices, Right Choices: Letting Students Speak

Throughout my experience serving in the armed forces, I was immersed in culture that both taught and embedded organization and structure into the daily routine. I knew that when my enlistment contract was finished, I wanted to find a job as a high school history teacher and utilize some of the same structure in my classroom. I believed that communication and structure were key elements for a successful educational environment.

Once I landed my first position, I used the traditional "cemetery seating" in my classroom. Cemetery seating is when all the student desks are lined up in orderly rows. I only intended to teach using direct instruction. I wasn't a fan of students working with partners or in groups, so I made sure my assignments were tailored to the individual student. My desire was for students to learn what it was that I was teaching them, and my initial approach was based on both my experiences in high school and the military.

For the most part, I found success in this approach. Every student that I ever taught passed the state standardized test in my subject area, and for that I prided myself on a job well done. I believed at the time that this was the mark of an effective educator. I was checking all the boxes on my annual evaluation, but I slowly realized that my students weren't climbing the progression of Bloom's Taxonomy. I began to wonder if my students really were just excellent at memorizing key facts, dates, and events in world history.

Now, as a school administrator, while I think there was some benefit to the processes I had in place in my classroom, I would secretly frown upon this approach today. I realize now I lacked creativity and innovation, and I very rarely integrated technology into my lessons. I interpreted being a firm teacher as being an effective teacher.

PATHWAY TO PARTICIPATION

We understand that, ideally, we should know more about our subject area than our students do, hence the reason the government has mandated schools and teachers. It's important that we share what we know, but we cannot leave out one of the most central elements: engaging the student. We must create ways for students of all learning styles to be able to learn what we are teaching.

Just like establishing culture in our classroom, where we might think our classroom environment feels one way only to find out our students feel differently, the same is true with our instruction. Just because we're confident in the material and in our delivery of the material—standing in front of our students and presenting them with written notes to copy from the board—doesn't mean that all learners actually learned.

There is a time and a place for traditional notes, especially for students in a college prep program. However, if we think back to when we were in junior high and high school, we can remember in which classes we had the most fun and from which assignments we learned the most. Chances are they were classes that involved hands-on activities, inquiry-based assignments, or even ones with those coveted field trips. When our students are focused on copying notes from the board, they are often so focused on making sure they copy the words correctly that they aren't paying attention to their significance.

As a teacher, when I used traditional notes, I ensured they were guided notes. This meant that the students had printed copies of the notes and had to "fill in the blanks" as we went along. Based on my own learning style, I was able to better focus on the material when I knew where the starting and stopping points were. If a student got off track in the middle of the notes, they could simply look at their neighbor's paper and not have to interrupt the entire class. My desire now is for students to listen more than they write.

When we include activities in our classrooms such as working with partners or small groups, it gives students the opportunity to express what they've learned. Often in this type of setting, students have to present their finished products to the class, which allows students to share. We often think the only path to learning is by our instruction, but we must not forget that students can also learn from each other.

While some questions and assignments will undoubtedly be concrete in nature, remember that those types of lessons don't allow for creativity and expression of thought. When we design lessons and units that are more abstract, yet still in alignment with the state standards, it allows us to see another side of our students.

As part of our student leadership development program, we conduct an exercise where we split up twenty students into five groups of four students each. We give each student four quarters, and they have to decide how they will spend them. Most groups create ways to grow the money, but the ways in which they plan to do so all differ. Most groups have the same mission and the same end goal in mind, but they all take different paths to get there, based on their experiences and their abilities.

The same approach should be true in education. I am now a firm believer in giving students the opportunity to let their voices be heard. By "voices," I'm not just referring to their audible voices, but I am referring to them expressing their feelings, thoughts, and responses in more than one traditional way—not, of course, by leaving class to join a picket line fighting for less homework and better school lunches!

When we integrate systems that include project-based and inquiry-based learning assignments into our classes, we are providing the opportunity for students to work to their fullest potential. When we provide students with a rubric that has one basic project on it and they have to follow the steps, they are going to reach a capacity level within each subsection we are grading them on. But if the opportunities are essentially endless for the project, we will be amazed at what our students can produce as we allow their voices to be heard and we stop limiting their opportunity for maximum growth.

STUDENT VOICES: CREATING THEIR OWN POLICIES

A few years into teaching, I decided to do away with classroom rules and instead create classroom expectations. *Rules* are often limiting, but *expectations* provide the opportunity for students to grow. They also help to establish a level of responsibility and maturity. I included the students in this process and allowed them to determine collectively, under my guidance, what the expectations should be. They also participated in determining what the consequences would be for not meeting each expectation. I had the final approval, just to ensure the decisions were fair and equitable.

I taught my students that when they have a voice in helping create policy and procedure, they do not have the right to later complain about it when they don't want to adhere to it. It keeps them accountable because they will remember the consequences since they were included in the process of creating them.

I'm referring to creating policies at the beginning of the year that will last for the duration of the year, not that a student gets to determine their consequence every time they fail to adhere to an expectation. I do like the idea of letting a student spin a wheel labeled with consequences, but I'm not sure how I would be able to get parental support for that!

We need to post and publish our classroom policies and consequences, making sure that both the principal and the parents are provided with a copy.

Another way we can include student voices in the classroom is by establishing a student council or a classroom council. Some schools have grade level student councils, and we should definitely support these types of organizations.

However, we can also create a council inside our classroom. This council can help decide which restaurant to stop at for lunch on our next field trip, or even which movie to show on reward day. While we most certainly can figure these things out on our own, when we give students the opportunity to have a voice, it allows them to take ownership of the culture in their classroom.

With ownership comes the opportunity for students to fully participate in student leadership. While there is great benefit in teaching and modeling leadership, there is no greater experience for students than when they can step up to the plate and engage in peer-to-peer leadership.

One idea that students in my school implemented was taking a spare locker and creating a "Suggestion

Locker." On the front of the locker was a magnetized container that included a pen and post-it notes. Students could write suggestions for the school on the post-it notes and slide them into the air vent of the locker door. The student council would unlock the locker and read through the suggestions at each of their meetings.

Some of the ideas included wanting the administration to do away with homework; others requested that we serve pizza for breakfast. The students even offered potential themes for the homecoming dance.

I work hard as a principal to implement as many of the suggestions as possible that are cost-friendly, and that I know students will actually appreciate. Obviously, I can't just change the start time of school, or the homework policy, in the middle of the school year, but I know that if I make incremental, yet noticeable changes, the students will realize that their voice matters, and that the administration takes their suggestions seriously.

Students want to be taken seriously, and one way that can happen is by implementing group discussions in the classroom where appropriate. It is important, though, to moderate the discussions in a way that makes students feel protected and comfortable enough to participate. For instance, if a student completely bashes a religious sect, and we know that one of our students in the class participates in that religious group, we then have to find a way to make sure the student doesn't feel threatened.

Establishing ground rules and writing them on the board so that students have a visual reminder before the group discussion starts is a great starting point. If we're grading the participation of each student in the discussion, taking point deductions when they violate the rules is one way we can ensure that students understand the magnitude of governing what they say. Students should be free to express their thoughts, but should not be permitted to do so at the expense of their peers. This is a life-skill that we hope will transcend the classroom and serve them well in their future.

We also have to remember that students will often model behavior and words they have heard from other people, including adults, and not just that of their friends. Students are not born with the innate ability to use profanity—those are learned words. Students aren't born with the ability to walk or to read, they are taught at a certain age how to do both. In a moderated setting, it then becomes our responsibility to make sure that they learn appropriate ways to make their voices heard and their feelings known, while staying within the guidelines of the discussion.

Even when students violate our rules structure, we should still treat them with dignity. The ultimate goal would be to have a conversation with the student and figure out how we can best help them improve their conduct and not repeat the same behavior. When they see that we mean business, but that we still care for them throughout the discipline process, trust is built. We want them to think, "I was wrong, but I know Mr. Mills has my back."

CREATING A CULTURE
OF CARING COMMUNICATION

Encouragement goes a long way. We never know what each of our students is dealing with, so we should always operate with a level of understanding and empathy, even while holding students accountable. In that setting, using words that educate and enlighten them will have a greater impact than using words that tear down and demean.

When students answer questions correctly, we should acknowledge them. When students adhere to our expectations, we should acknowledge them. When students show kindness toward their peers, we should acknowledge them.

We should never publicly embarrass a student for not executing a task as instructed. Instead, we should find an appropriate time to address the issue and do so in a manner that will allow the student to learn from their mistake. When we operate from a place of care and love, students will know and feel the genuineness of our intent.

When students make positive life choices based on words of encouragement we have spoken to them, we have then had an influence and made an impact that will potentially change their lives forever. That is a goal worth working toward.

FOLLOW-UP QUESTIONS:
CHAPTER SEVENTEEN

1. Is your physical classroom set up in a manner that allows students to learn by engaging with their peers?

2. Think back to your last two or three lessons. Who did the most talking—you or your students? What kind of changes could you make that would allow for more student interaction and engagement?

3. What are two practical ways you allow students to express themselves in your daily routine?

4. When you think critically about the words you use in your classroom during your instruction and beyond, how do your students feel after you speak to them? Do they feel deflated? Inferior? Or do they feel motivated and energized—like they can tackle any project and succeed?

Chapter Eighteen

Everybody Wins, but Everybody Doesn't Get a Trophy

When I was in middle school, my principal created a program called "Conflict Managers" which consisted of students who had been trained to mediate peer-to-peer conflicts that arose on the playground. The students who participated as conflict managers were equipped with vests and clipboards. Their mission was to help the teachers make sure the playground was a safe environment for all students. In essence, they needed to make sure all the students were happy.

As educators, we too, often operate as conflict managers, but in the realm of making sure we operate with inclusion by including all of our students and their myriad of learning styles in our instruction. We must strive to make sure that our lesson plans include elements of differentiation based on the learning needs of the students we teach. This process will take creativity and patience, but it's absolutely needed and necessary for the growth of our students. If our students aren't growing, then what is our purpose as educators?

RAISE THE STANDARD

Each relationship we have in our lives requires a certain combination of time and energy. Those who have more than one child know that every child is different—they each have different desires and require different care, but all deserve to be treated with fairness.

The same is true with our students. The interactions we have with our students will all vary based on what it is the students need. Our interaction, when it comes to academic needs and behavioral needs, will vary based on the situation of each student.

Regardless of the conditions, though, we must hold the bar high and continue to raise the standard for that student. Integrating rigor into our lessons doesn't just apply to the highest achieving students in the class, but to all students. We can't let students use their differences as a crutch for making excuses. Instead, we can use their differences as a way to challenge them to achieve even more.

In all decisions, we must work to make sure there is benefit for the student, not for us. For instance, when it comes to student discipline in the classroom, our goal is always to redirect behavior, not to punish it. If we ever get to the point where we want to "get even" with a student, it might be time to consider a career change or to re-evaluate our mission statement and see what we can do in order to stay in alignment with our purpose of existence as an educator.

THE SOCIALISM SAGA

Think back to high school or college: were you ever required to work on a group project, and it seemed like you were doing all the work? You were worried the night before the project was due, so you started texting the other group members to make sure their parts were finished. You were mentally prepared for how all the parts would sync together. You arrived at school the next morning with your presentation prepared and found that the effort your peers put forth was minimal—and it showed. You were worried that your grade was going to drop due to their lack of preparedness, only to realize that not only did your group overall get a good grade, but that the entire group got the same grade!

In a scenario like this, it's only natural for us to become frustrated. Unfortunately, this is part of life. In education, there will be times when we feel like we're holding the entire department together, yet the principal seems to always acknowledge the entire group, or maybe just the tenured teacher.

Inside, we know that we have worked the hardest and deserved the recognition and the credit. While someone will inevitably emerge as a leader in group settings, we must remember that in these types of environments, all parties must strive to work together for the common good. There are some instances where certain people will work harder than others, but that's the nature of the game. I wish there were a magic formula to fix this, but there just isn't.

One way to ensure that we include the feedback of all people in a group is to solicit feedback from everyone in the group. In our school, as in most schools, we have student groups and organizations. Within these groups, there are council members or officers. While we expect that the faculty adviser will make sure that the students are meeting their group objectives, we also place a significant amount of responsibility into the hands of the student leaders. If we have to tell the students what to do or what to think, then we're managing them, not leading them, and it's not our job to manage, but to lead.

I've been involved in a lot of conflict resolutions during my years as an educator. Some of these situations arose because certain students didn't feel like their views or feedback were being received by the other students or student leaders.

When students are voted into or appointed to leadership positions for the first time, there is often a steep learning curve and a lot of training involved. I think we often like the idea of leadership, but don't realize that the application of leadership requires a specific set of thoughts and actions. Leadership is harder than it looks!

HOMECOMING DANCE: SPANISH LUAU?

One situation in particular that I recall is when the students on the Homecoming Dance committee

212

couldn't come to a mutual agreement on the theme. I brought the group into my office and allowed each student to share their view and their ideas. The room was split into several groups as far as the desired theme was concerned.

One group wanted a luau, another wanted a fiesta, and the other wanted a "Night in the Park." I never understood what was so exciting about being in the park at night, but I digress. Because the students were working so hard at putting the dance together and were creating so much excitement leading up to the event, I wanted to somehow include elements of all their ideas.

In essence, I wanted everybody to win. Not every person's ideas were going to be a grand slam and earn them the MVP trophy, but everyone was going to have sufficient feedback that would allow all the group members to at least get on base and stay in the game. That was the goal of my meeting.

Long story short, the students eventually agreed on a theme. They were able to successfully implement all their themes and ideas into the overall concept of the dance. The dance was a luau by theme, but it included a piñata, and a taco and pizza bar.

To be honest, the students had so much fun, they didn't even realize that the different theme and décor elements didn't mesh well together. It was certainly brightly decorated, and the music was a hit, as always. In this situation, everybody won. This approach works wonders in conflict resolution when the disagreement simply stems from several people not being able to come to a decision.

While we can't and won't make everyone happy all the time, we must work to make sure we are making the best decisions for the students in our classrooms. Taking inventory and reflecting can bring tremendous opportunities for our students. Making sure that all students are respected and permitted to engage in the communication and learning process in our classrooms yields a level of respect and cooperation that will ultimately benefit both students and educators.

Remember those short videos on social media where a father is all dressed up and playing tea party with his youngest daughter? I could almost guarantee that wasn't the first item on the father's "to-do" list that day, but I could guarantee that was probably one of the most rewarding and fulfilling moments of his day. What might seem insignificant to us might mean the absolute world to our students.

In some cases, small wins and small victories will feel like our students have won the Super Bowl. In these moments, we should celebrate. We can't wait for the big moments because they show up too few and far between. When students are encouraged on their journey and know they are loved and cared for, they will often continue on their journey, no matter how hard it may seem, because they know success is on the way.

It is up to us to find a way to acknowledge progress. While every student won't finish as the valedictorian or earn a 100% on every unit test, every student does have the opportunity to increase in knowledge. It is up to us to encourage them to achieve more, to do more, and to become more, both in the classroom and beyond.

FOLLOW-UP QUESTIONS:
CHAPTER EIGHTEEN

1. What are the appropriate steps to take when you can't find resolution for an on-going issue with a student in your classroom?

2. How can you make sure every student in your classroom "wins" when it comes to their academic progress?

3. What are some practical ways you can celebrate "wins" in the classroom that don't cost you a lot of money, but make your students feel like a million bucks?

CONCLUSION

Pick Up the Phone!

One of the most challenging realities of education is that the majority of the issues we deal with on a daily or ongoing basis were not covered in the college classes we attended. Field experience and student-teaching are helpful, but they often lack the opportunity for genuine connection with students. Many college curriculums do not yet prepare us for the varied demographics of our students. An improved understanding of demographics would undoubtedly help us develop relationships with our students, since each demographic typically requires a distinct approach and a unique set of skills.

In this book, I told the story of one of my former students named Judah. On paper, Judah and I had nothing in common. I often felt that if we'd had more in common, I would have been better suited to help him during one of the roughest periods of his life. I think we will always look back and question whether anything we've done has truly made an impact on our students. I often wonder if my attempts at helping students and pushing them into their purpose have succeeded.

We will also have those challenging times in our career when we simply won't know what to do in certain situations. I'm not an overly emotional person, but I do have compassion when I see a student in need, and I will reach out to do what I can.

Judah was experiencing a wide range of emotions as he dealt with changes in his living situation, the passing of his mother, and the challenge of maintaining good grades so he could successfully transition to college.

I remember the day he called to say he was on his way back home—he had received word that his mother didn't have long to live. I left work early that day so I could meet him and drive him to the hospice facility.

Judah has a strong interest in music, and a desire to pursue it. On the way to the facility, he connected his phone to the radio in my car and turned on a song he had written and recorded. Honestly, I didn't know what I could say to comfort or encourage him, so we drove in silence and just listened to his music.

Shortly before we arrived, there was a passage in his song that caught me off guard. He had included an actual voicemail from his mother—her very last one to him—in the song. In the voicemail, she said, "Judah, it's your mom. Pick up the phone. Please call me back."

Judah began to cry when he heard her voice. He knew two things: he didn't have many more hours left with his mother, and he wished he would have picked up the phone that day.

If there is a lesson I have learned from my interactions with Judah, it is this: we will only have these students in our classrooms for a few, short months, or in our schools for a few, short years. We will never know how great an impact we might have on them by simply taking the time to *Pick Up the Phone*.

Printed in Great Britain
by Amazon